The voice of the Awakening

Constance K. Walker

EP PUBLISHING WITH A MISSION

EP BOOKS
Faverdale North
Darlington
DL3 0PH, England

www.epbooks.org
sales@epbooks.org

EP BOOKS are distributed in the USA by:
JPL Fulfillment
3741 Linden Avenue Southeast,
Grand Rapids, MI 49548.

E-mail: sales@jplfulfillment.com
Tel: 877.683.6935

First published 2013

British Library Cataloguing in Publication Data available
ISBN: 978-0-85234-957-1

Adolphe Monod

Contents

	Page
Monod genealogy	6
Preface	7
1 Fear and trembling	11
2 The calling	17
3 Cross-currents	29
4 Crisis and victory	49
5 Testing by fire	69
6 Breaking new ground	93
7 A voice for evangelicals	117
8 Preaching and pain	139
9 Farewells	161
Further reading	171
Sources	173

Monod genealogy

Jean Monod (1765–1836) = Louise de Coninck (1775–1851)
|

Frédéric Monod (1794–1863)   = Constance de Coninck
                                  = Suzanne Smedley
Henri Monod (1795–1869)   = Camille Gros
Adèle Monod (1796–1876)   = Édouard Babut (1787–1848)
Édouard Monod (1798–1887)   = Elisa Gros
Guillaume (Billy) Monod   = Sophie Peschier-Vieusseux
    (1800–1896)   = Nina Lauront
Adolphe Monod   = Hannah Honyman(1799–1868)
    (21 Jan 1802–6 Apr 1856)
                           |

      Mary Monod (29 May 1831–1890)   = Henri Morin
      Louise Marguerite Monod
         (8 Nov 1832–1887)   = Auguste Bouvier
      André John William Monod
         (29 Aug 1834–1916)   = Marie Vallette
      Sarah Monod (24 Jun 1836–1912)
      Emilie Monod (24 Apr 1838–1920)   = Théodore Audeoud
      Constance Monod (22 Aug 1840–26 Sep 1841)
      Camille Monod (20 Oct 1843–1910)   = Charles Félix Vernes

Gustave Monod (1803–1890)   = Jane Good
Valdemar Monod (1807–1870)   = Adèle le Cavelier
Marie Suzanne Monod (1809–1886)   = Charles-Louis Stapfer
Edmond Monod (1813–1813)
Horace Monod (1814–1881)   = Suzanne Gardes
Elisa Monod (1815–1867)
Marie Cécile Elizabeth (Betsy) Monod (1818–?)

Preface

Adolphe Monod (1802–1856) was a beloved and courageous French pastor, a major figure in the nineteenth-century Awakening. While he is still well-known among our French-speaking brothers, most English-speaking evangelicals have scarcely heard of him. My prayer is that this short biography will help make this humble and passionate servant of Christ better known.

Since my conversion in 1975, many Christians from our own and earlier eras have contributed to the growth and orientation of my faith, yet none has done so more broadly or consistently than Adolphe Monod. I first made his acquaintance in the stacks of Duke University's Perkins Library. I was searching for Christian books in French as a way of building up my faith while maintaining the linguistic skills I had gained while working at a research laboratory outside Paris. (Yes, I'm a scientist.) In God's providence and through an odd set of circumstances, I 'stumbled' upon a dusty, seemingly obscure volume from 1856 containing

Monod's death-bed meditations. Some of the chapter titles looked sombre and depressing, but I was desperate and checked the book out.

Once I began to read *Les Adieux* (or *Farewells*), I realized that the titles given to the meditations were often misleading, having been chosen by Monod's children as they watched his health ebbing away. The meditations themselves were filled with life and peace and often joy, even as the speaker was suffering from intense, unremitting pain. Beyond that, the messages displayed a beautiful balance between logic and feeling, between appeals to the head and to the heart. Monod set out a lofty standard for the Christian life, while managing to make that standard winsomely appealing. His wisdom was profound. I was captivated. Only much later did I discover that Adolphe Monod was actually the most famous and beloved French-speaking evangelical pastor of his day and that *Les Adieux* is a classic work in francophone countries.

Les Adieux was thus the beginning of my decades-long 'friendship' with Adolphe Monod. I have now read and pondered many of his published works. I have also translated and edited *Les Adieux* and four books of his sermons (see Further reading). Each volume has its own special character, and each is a challenging, thought-provoking delight. Monod's sermons display the same wonderful qualities I found in his *Farewells*, but with a more thorough and extended exposition of the author's thoughts.

I can see why Monod was called 'the voice of the Awakening'. His impact was enormous, as he laboured to awaken the nominal Christians of his era to a living, vibrant, personal faith in Jesus Christ and as he challenged those who had such faith to live more wholeheartedly for their Saviour. The richness of his classic, romantic prose is only matched by the richness of his thought and the depth of his love for his Saviour.

But how did God prepare Adolphe Monod for his work, and how did he fashion his faith? What natural gifts did he put into him, and what natural weaknesses did he permit in order to force his servant to lean more fully on him? And how did he lead Monod into his appointed ministry? That, of course, is the subject of this book. As believers in Christ, the work assigned to each of us is different, but the qualities of faith and character the Lord seeks to form in us and the ways he guides us are similar. And so, in researching and crafting this biography, I have found the story of Adolphe Monod's life to be almost as powerful and touching as his writings.

As the book nears completion, I am grateful for the many people who commented on the essay from which it evolved. Special thanks go to William Edgar for his linguistic and cultural insights and to Michael Haykin, who was courageous enough to entrust this biography to a scientist. Finally, Graham Hind and the staff at EP have been a blessing and an encouragement to me through the enthusiasm, sensitivity, and care with which they have embraced this project. My efforts have been bathed in much prayer, and I have often sensed a divine enabling that has left me humble and grateful. Even though imperfections undoubtedly remain in the final product, this has been a joyful work of love. May it profit many in the family of God.

1
Fear and trembling
(1855)

Pentecost was approaching, and the minister in Paris prayed fervently as he prepared his sermon.

Oh, who will grant me understanding of what I should explain to your people? My soul sighs after you, oh my God, and my spirit prays within me with inarticulate sighs. ... Do I dare say that the gift of the Holy Spirit surpasses even that of the Son, not in love but in breadth? This is the goal towards which the cross itself is only the pathway. ... If the veil is torn, it is in order to open the Holy of Holies. If Jesus' flesh has been bruised, it is in order to open heaven for us and cause it to come down into our hearts. Oh, cloudless certainty! Oh, boundless rejoicing! Oh, perfect conformity to Christ! Oh, unshadowed light! Oh, Satan crushed beneath our feet! Oh, Christ with us and in us! Oh, all the fullness of the Godhead poured out on humanity! My God, open my eyes, my heart, and my lips!

Do you hear his heart cry? Do you sense the depth of his love for his Saviour? Do you see his humility and his utter dependence on God?

This prayer of humble dependence did not come from a novice minister, a recent seminary graduate full of fresh love for God yet anxiously preparing one of his first sermons. This was Adolphe Monod (pronounced *Ah-Dolf Moh-Noh*), the most famous and beloved French-speaking Protestant preacher of his day, at the very height of his preaching ability. No, the dependence and humility we hear in this prayer reveal not Monod's inexperience but the very strength of his ministry. He knew his source of supply, and he knew that it did not lie within himself. It lay within the riches of the God whom he served so faithfully. He was totally dependent on the Holy Spirit who came down at Pentecost.

Monod's preaching pulpit in Paris

Though he didn't know it, this was to be the last time Adolphe Monod would climb the steps to the preaching pulpit in Paris. At age fifty-three, his health was deteriorating rapidly, and he was preparing to take an extended leave of absence.

During those months, his health continued to decline, and his suffering increased. On Pentecost he had acknowledged that God might not heal him; now that seemed more and more likely.

My God, you want to test what is in my heart. You want to see if this old servant, who has preached with great power and conviction that there is nothing over which faith cannot triumph, is prepared to prove it himself. You want to see if he accepts the burden that he has placed on the shoulders of others. I accept this burden. I know that it is you who sends me this awful suffering, who sustains it, who prolongs it. I know that you are my Father, that you are goodness itself, and that you will send me deliverance, whether by healing me or by withdrawing me to your bosom. ...

Hurry! Distance me from all anxiety for the future. I am sometimes frightened by the slowness of this disease. I am frightened by the prospect of what lies ahead of me. But no, you are love. You are faithful. You have now given me the crucified life I so often desired in my times of health, and I accept it so as to demonstrate that the Christian can, indeed, find peace in this crucified life.

Though faith battles fear in these words, ultimately he found deep peace. It was in September that the family finally learned that Adolphe Monod's illness was terminal liver cancer. Six long months of suffering lay ahead. Deprived of his public ministry, he was soon giving a series of short weekly meditations to friends and family. These 'farewells' were written down by his children and published just after his death. Filled with life and peace and even joy, they have become a classic in French Evangelical literature. Listen to part of the last meditation, given just one week before his death. His title was 'God is Love'; his text was Psalm 100, a joyful song of praise. The meditation moved rapidly to prayer.

Your goodness, your goodness! My God, I give you thanks for how gratuitously that goodness is demonstrated in freely pardoning me for all of my faults; me, the chief among sinners, the least of your children, the poorest of your servants; but also me whom you have filled with blessings and used for the advancement of your reign even in the excess of weakness and pain in which I am plunged today! …

I want it to be known that there is nothing in me capable of surviving for one moment before the brightness of your face and before the light of your holiness. But now it is not I who will be judged, it is Christ in me; and I know, I know that he will enter, and I with him, and that he and I are so fully united that he would never enter and leave me outside. …

It is true, Lord, for I desire to be sincere before you, that I suffer much, and that my joy and my thanksgiving are made sombre by these continual sufferings and exhaustion. But you have sustained me up to this point, and I am confident that my prayers and those of my family and friends will win for me perfect patience. …

> *Oh, my God, sanctify us perfectly, and may all that remains to us of life be employed totally in your service. May your Spirit dwell in us and be the soul, the life, and the joy of us all.*

His faith prevailed, but forging the steel of that faith from an inherited religion was a painful process. During more than six years of confusion and then crisis, as God was weaning Adolphe Monod from trust in his own intellect and hard work, he used many human agents. Some were family members, especially Adolphe's eldest brother and eldest sister. Yet on his death-bed, there were three men he especially wanted to thank for their role in his conversion. Their contributions were different and complementary, each adding to the full-orbed, balanced Christian faith that characterized Adolphe Monod's ministry. Louis Gaussen, a Genevan cousin and evangelical pastor, contributed to the *precision* of Monod's doctrine; Charles Scholl, the pastor of the French Protestant Church in London, contributed *practicality* to his ministry; and Thomas Erskine, a Scottish lay evangelist, imparted a *passion* to his love for the Saviour. The story of Adolphe Monod's life is the story of how God used these men and others to help fashion a vibrant evangelical faith, how God tested and refined that faith through trial, and then how he used it to sustain a broad and powerful ministry within the renewal movement stirring nineteenth-century French-speaking Protestantism. It is the story of how his humble servant became 'the voice of the Awakening'.

2

The calling

(1802–1820)

The Kanin-Gaard estate was a wonderful place for a young boy to grow up, and there Adolphe Monod spent much of his first seven years. Situated on the shores of Lake Fuür on the outskirts of Copenhagen, Kanin-Gaard's vast acreage boasted of fruit orchards, rabbits, cows, and a herd of sheep, complete with a ram. A nearby and much grander estate was occupied by doting and wealthy grandparents. Dronning-Gaard had a variety of gardens and a vast park where imported antelope roamed between trees brought from overseas by Adolphe's maternal grandfather, Frédéric de Coninck. Boats, including miniature but accurate warships, were available for recreation and games on the lake. What more could a boy want?

Kanin-Gaard

Beginnings

On his father's side, Adolphe Monod came from a prominent family of Swiss Protestants from the Geneva area. His grandfather, Gaspard-Joël Monod (1717–1782), was ordained in Geneva, spent thirteen years as a family tutor in Holland, and served for four years as pastor of the French Reformed Church in Guadeloupe, before returning to Geneva. At the age of forty-seven, he married Adolphe's grandmother, Suzanne-Madeleine Puerari, age twenty-seven. Joël did not resume his pastoral duties. They lived on a small Puerari-family estate near Geneva, leaving Joël free to supervise the education of the children and pursue an interest in literature.

Adolphe's father, Jean Monod (1765–1836), was the first of their three children and followed his father into the Calvinist ministry, taking his seminary training in Geneva.

He met Louise de Coninck while spending a few months in Copenhagen. Her father, Frédéric, was a prosperous and prominent merchant who often opened his home to visitors. Jean, then aged twenty-six, was one of them and soon won the heart of sixteen-year-old Louise. Jean returned to Geneva, but the following year, 1792, saw him back in Copenhagen, preaching in the French Reformed Church there. A few months later, just following Louise's seventeenth birthday, the two were married and began their life together in Geneva.

Not long after the birth of their first son — named Frédéric, after Louise's father — Jean was called to Copenhagen to become one of the pastors of the Reformed Church. He served that congregation from 1794 to 1808. His father-in-law had established Kanin-Gaard for the use of his younger son but made it available to the Monods. There the family grew to include seven sons and a daughter. One maid and eventually a second helped Louise run the household.

Louise Monod

Adolphe-Louis-Frédéric-Théodore Monod, their sixth child and fifth son, was born on 21 January 1802. Two years later, a young Swiss pastor was hired to supervise the children's education. There was, as might be expected, a certain amount of boyish mischief, largely organized by Frédéric. A large cherry tree bore good fruit on one side and rather poor fruit on the other. The boys were authorized to climb the tree to pick some of the inferior cherries, but it was often suspected that they made 'mistakes' in their selection. They were also allowed to go into the garden in early morning to gather any fruit that had fallen overnight. One day, Adolphe was caught shaking a tree to encourage a better harvest!

Paris

The peace and charm of this existence ended shortly after hostilities broke out between England and Denmark, disrupting Frédéric de Coninck's commerce and leading the Monods to leave Copenhagen. Ten years earlier, in 1798, Jean's preaching had attracted the attention of the consistory, or ruling church body, of the Reformed Church in Paris. When one of their pastors died prematurely, Jean was called to replace him. Given the waning fortunes of the de Coninck family and Jean's concern for the further education of his children, he accepted the position with the blessing of his in-laws.

The journey to Paris wasn't easy. Their company was large, Louise was five months pregnant with her ninth child, and the British had a naval blockade of Denmark in effect. The ship carrying the Monods was chased by a British vessel and took refuge in an island port for several days before it could evade pursuit and get the family to Germany. From there a month-long land voyage took them to Paris.

Paris was not Kanin-Gaard, but neither was it the crowded metropolis of today. It had its own charms. From the end of 1808 throughout the remainder of Adolphe's childhood, the family occupied a series of rented apartments with large gardens, again often with fruit trees. In their first dwelling on Rue Pigalle, the children's bedroom was a former sky-lit picture gallery, in which a stove was installed for heating. Then for nine years they occupied the more spacious quarters of a three-storey house on the Rue d'Hauteville. Shortly before Adolphe left to pursue his studies in Geneva, the family moved to what was once a hunting lodge of Louis XV on Rue de la Tour-d'Auvergne, on the edge of Paris, bordering Montmartre and practically in the countryside. Its 'garden' was two and a half acres, allowing the family to grow more than enough fruits and vegetables for their own use, and even to raise chickens.

In Paris the family grew to include twelve children — eight sons and four daughters — plus a ninth son who lived only a few months. Without the sustained financial help of Louise's father, Jean Monod's income as a pastor was inadequate to support such a large family. Therefore, they accepted boarders or pensioners, most of them young men whose education Jean supervised along with the education of his own children. Around six more boys, mostly from wealthy families, were added to the household at any given time.

From their earliest years, Adolphe and his brother Guillaume — known to everyone as Billy — were inseparable companions. When they were sixteen and eighteen, respectively, their older sister, Adèle, wrote what she entitled

Portraits of the Twelve Sparrows, describing herself and her siblings. Each sibling has his own portrait … except for Adolphe and Billy, who were combined.

> They are so united that they seem to form but one *between them, and that* one *is perfect, because they correct one another's faults and give one another their good qualities.*
>
> Billy communicates his angelic sweetness to Adolphe, and he, in turn, inspires a firmness of character that is otherwise lacking in his brother. Billy is more exact, more precise; Adolphe is livelier and has more finesse. Putting these qualities together, it can be imagined that they work very well, because they always work together. … Each has a high opinion of the other's talents.

Oddly, though Billy was the elder of the two, apparently it was Adolphe who made most of the decisions.

Among the other siblings, two played especially large roles in Adolphe's life and spiritual growth: his eldest brother, Frédéric, who served as a spiritual mentor, and his eldest sister, Adèle, who understood her brother well and whose deep faith and fervent prayers were crucial in ending his spiritual crisis.

Within the family Adolphe was noted for his lively intelligence, for his cheerfulness, and for being easy to get along with. He also had a passion for games, especially games of skill. But above all, he seems to have been a perfectionist, wanting to excel and distinguish himself.

A rigorous education

Part of any boy's existence is education, and in Paris this took many forms. Jean Monod, who was one of two and later three pastors in the Reformed Church of Paris, personally supervised the religious education of the children. For their remaining studies he hired a tutor. The first two were unable to maintain discipline with the older boys, who had brought disruptive habits with them from Copenhagen. Jean then decided to send Frédéric (the chief trouble-maker?) to Geneva to live as a pensioner with a pastor friend, and he hired Mr Küster, a young pastor from Hanover, Germany, to instruct his remaining children. Tall, thin, and vigorous, Mr Küster was able to subdue his young charges more by affection than by severity, though he was still quite rigorous.

He made sure that the children had regular physical exercise in addition to their mental exercise, and in his desire to harden them to discomfort, their schoolroom at the house was typically unheated in the early morning hours, even in winter. Yet the boys were expected to get up at six a.m. and work until the tutor's arrival at eight o'clock, completing assignments left for them the night before. On one occasion the ink was frozen in the inkwells! Mr Küster made his students work hard, while also instilling in them a keen desire to learn. The principal subjects he taught were Greek, Latin, German, English, Italian, history and geography. The sciences were studied at the Collège Bourbon. Other subjects were taken at the Sorbonne, the Collège de France, and the Bibliothèque Royale.

Jean Monod

The children's education continued even during extended vacations. The Monod family was well connected, and the children were often invited to spend time at a country residence of family friends. A favourite place was Auchy-les-Moines, due north of Paris and close to the Belgian border. The lovely, spacious home at Auchy was associated with a cotton-spinning mill that had been built on the grounds of an old monastery. Two days of travel by horse-drawn carriage brought students and tutor to the town of Abbeville. The third day they would ride on a cart that carried bales of cotton to the mill, arriving at midday at Auchy.

The vacations might last more than two months. Mornings were devoted to studies, but afternoons were free for excursions in the surrounding area. Another favourite occupation was producing and performing plays — making the costumes, studying their lines, and rehearsing their roles. One of those plays was a tragedy called *Les Templiers*, which had first been produced by the Comédie Française in 1805. When Billy and Adolphe wrote a parody in verse of *Les Templiers*, the children produced that as well. There was no shortage of impish fun.

A formal but sincere faith

The family faith that Jean taught to his children is hard to define. Some assessments link it too much to liberalism and fail to capture the reverence in which both God and his Word were held. Others make it sound as if it were already influenced by the spiritual Awakening, or *Réveil*, which swept into French-speaking Switzerland and on into France beginning around 1815. Perhaps the best assessment portrays French Protestantism of the period as overtaken by spiritual slumber following decades of persecution. The Reformation had a troubled history in France, complicated in later years by political instability. All this had left its mark on the French Reformed Church.

The period from 1562 to 1598 was characterized by what are called the 'Wars of Religion'. These ended when Henry IV issued the Edict of Nantes, granting religious toleration and restoring civil rights to the Huguenots — or Calvinist French Protestants — within what was still a largely Roman Catholic country. The edict remained in effect until 1685, when it was revoked by Henry's grandson, Louis XIV. Numerous Huguenot families, including Louise Monod's de Coninck ancestors, fled France in fear. Many went to The Netherlands, Switzerland, and Great Britain; some went as far as South Africa and North America. Things changed again with the French Revolution, which began in 1789. This led to a period of political instability that continued throughout Adolphe Monod's lifetime. For the Protestant church, however, the big breakthrough came in 1802 when the Organic Articles were promulgated under the government known as The Consulate. The Organic Articles gave official recognition to the French Reformed Church and affirmed, as its doctrinal standards, the Bible and the 1559 confession of faith known as *The Confession of La Rochelle*. The Articles also made the government responsible for approving the appointment and dismissal of pastors, paying their salaries, determining the number and location of Protestant houses of worship (referred to as 'temples'), and appointing members of the local churches' ruling bodies, called consistories.

In the ensuing years, many Calvinist French Protestants held the Bible and the traditional Calvinist doctrinal standards in great reverence out of respect for their ancestors, yet they were weary and unwilling to examine those standards, perhaps for fear that, if they questioned them, they might dishonour their heritage. This state, sometimes termed *supranaturalism*, could easily apply to the Monods, especially given Louise's Huguenot ancestry.

The faith of the Monod family appears to have been sincere but without real depth or life, pious but formal. The basic tenets of the Reformation — salvation by grace, Christ's redeeming work, and the need for repentance, new birth, and sanctification — were not denied; they were acknowledged but not really understood. The emphasis was on living a godly life, on 'working out your own salvation with fear and trembling' with no recognition that this requires leaning on 'God who works in you both to will and to work for his good pleasure' (Philippians 2:12-13). Jean and Louise passed this heritage on to their children.

Though lacking warmth and life, this formal godliness had a large impact on the children. Four of the eight sons went into the pastorate, and Adolphe was called to the ministry when he was only fourteen years old. His poem *My Calling* was written to his parents on the occasion of his fifteenth birthday. The middle stanza shows the nature of his youthful faith.

> *World, 'tis not thee whose air I inhale.*
> *My heart finds no hope in that which must fail.*
> *Wealth, glory, honours, flee far from my gaze,*
> *For I know your great greed and your dangerous ways.*
> *From your treacherous traps, he will rescue my soul;*
> *It is him, him alone, whose ways I would know.*
> *Taken up with his laws, my desire and my care:*
> *To lead Christians my love for the Saviour to share;*
> *To walk in the steps of the dearest of fathers,*
> *And devote myself fully to saving my brothers.*
> *Christians, dear flock, I am your shepherd;*
> *Come, follow me to the house of the Lord.*
> *Poor and afflicted, come there to find grace,*
> *And come seek a cure your grief to erase.*
> *Rich, learn to merit your wealth and your fame;*
> *Righteous, come join me in praising God's name.*
> *Sinners, come learn of a Father's true love.*
> *Oh, if through great goodness bestowed from above,*
> *This God would allow me to lead unto him*
> *A brother in sadness and hardened by crime,*
> *Oh, what gladness, what transports of joy would be mine!*

It would be easy to dismiss this poem as youthful enthusiasm inspired by the examples of his father and older brother. The next stanza makes their influence quite explicit, and even in the stanza above we see the mention of walking 'in the steps of the dearest of fathers'. In addition, a year earlier, Adolphe had written a laudatory letter to Frédéric, who was studying at the seminary in Geneva.

> *Every day I gain a greater taste for the path I must follow, above all when I hear a good sermon, and particularly since the discourse I heard you give. All my desires are directed towards equalling you. You will, perhaps, say that this is to aim a bit too high, but I hope, with a great deal of effort, to succeed. … I wish for all your discourses the same success that crowned your first efforts.*

Yet something much deeper than admiration must have been going on. An unshakeable sense of calling remained on Adolphe Monod's heart even, as we shall see, in the midst of a deep spiritual crisis that went on for years. One is forced to conclude that his sense of calling was, indeed, from God, who had his own purposes for this young life. Those purposes would be brought about and fulfilled through trial.

3

Cross-currents

(1820–1824)

Geneva beckoned. The year was 1820, and it was time for Adolphe and Billy to leave the family circle. The brothers were intent on becoming ministers of the gospel, and there was really no question as to where they would pursue their studies. Family tradition and family ties both pointed to the lovely city of Geneva.

Geneva is sheltered by the Alps and the Jura mountains as it embraces Lac Léman (or Lake Geneva) where the Rhône River flows out of it heading south. It was also the home of the Faculté de Théologie, where Adolphe's father, Jean, had been trained, receiving ordination in 1787. Frédéric had likewise studied there and was ordained in 1818. A French Protestant seminary founded in Montauban in 1808 was still not as highly regarded as its Swiss counterpart. Beyond the academic considerations, Jean had grown up in the region around Geneva, so there were many relatives and family friends who were prepared to welcome the young students.

Jean was to travel with his two sons, and their trip was delayed when he fell ill. Thus it was only in early November 1820 that the party arrived at the seminary. Adolphe was just eighteen years old; Billy was twenty.

Geneva on Lac Léman

Life in Geneva

The presence of family and friends, including Jean Monod's brother and sister, certainly eased the personal adjustment to leaving home. The young men stayed with their aunt, Mrs de Coutouly, who made every effort to provide a comfortable room and abundant hospitality for them. There were so many natural associations, and they were so warmly received that Adolphe and Billy had to limit the number of social engagements they would accept. They had studies to pursue.

The boys had also promised to send their mother an open and complete account of their time in seminary.

> *Here, dear Mama, is the beginning of the journal that you asked us for. But not every day is a holiday, so you should not expect that we will spend one or two hours a day filling up long pages here. We can give it very little time; yet you need only recall the aim of this journal to understand that it doesn't require much time. Each evening, before we go to bed, we will take turns writing here, in just a few words, the events of the day, down to the smallest details, even down to our most intimate troubles and pleasures, our contentment, our reproaches, our most secret feelings. By 'secret', I mean that which we would not even confide to our most intimate friends. Yet where it concerns our parents, our beloved parents, we have nothing to hide, and this journal will be the proof of it. This good mother has promised to read with interest all these little details, and how would it not be a true pleasure for us to converse every day with her in this way and to open the secrets of our hearts to her?*

What precious insights flow from those pages! Louise, in return, wrote to them frequently with amusing details of family life in Paris. Her letters, written sometimes in French, sometimes in English, were whimsically addressed to Mr B. A. Monod (i.e., Billy Adolphe Monod). Their father's letters were less frequent and more serious, occasionally advising them with regard to their studies.

The brothers soon found themselves delighted not just with family and friends, but with Geneva itself. While still in the family home, they had studied mathematics and science at the Collège Bourbon; now they were interacting with scientists. A year after their arrival Adolphe wrote:

> When I see the naturalists [biologists?], physicists, and all these distinguished scientists, I am tempted to envy the lot of those who come to Geneva to study the sciences. Here they find so many resources, so many learned and obliging men that so long as they can avoid the dangers of Geneva's dissipation, they could not be better off than here. I cannot say as much for philosophy. Certainly we have nothing here to compare with what Paris offers.

Then, during their last year of studies, he wrote in the journal for his mother:

> If you were not in Paris with all that I hold most dear in the world, I would be Swiss, heart and soul. This unique country unites all that could be found elsewhere of what is great and rich and lovely. In the midst of general worry and sadness, peace and tranquility still reign in this happy corner of the earth. Finally, for us in particular, the welcome we received in Geneva has been so good and so friendly — and due less to ourselves than to the name we bear — that we will never forget the family and friends that we will leave here, just as I hope we will never be forgotten.

Theological studies

The academic adjustment to Geneva was also fairly easy. The brothers passed their entrance examinations and from the beginning enjoyed the good graces of their professors, who had favourable memories of Frédéric. The students were also diligent and used to hard work, thanks to the training of their father and Mr Küster.

Classes at the Faculty of Theology were small. There were only four other young men in Adolphe and Billy's class, and they had four professors. One taught Hebrew, plus Old and New Testament; one taught pastoral theology, homiletics (the preparation and delivery of sermons), and apologetics; the third gave instruction in 'dogma'; and the fourth covered church history. Presumably the students were already proficient in Greek. The first two professors put a lot of emphasis on recitation and improvisation — that is, on the art of public speaking. For one, they recited mainly poetry, for the other mainly prose. Each May, the seminary students had to pass general exams administered by the company of Geneva pastors. The

Billy and Adolphe Monod as young men

first year, Billy ranked first among the students tested, with Adolphe a close second. In subsequent years the brothers consistently received the highest marks.

Recognizing the limitations of the seminary curriculum, they set about to supplement it. They took Arabic lessons on the side and helped organize a group of students who met for extra practice in reading and composition. Then, as if not busy enough, they took their father's advice and offered tutoring on the side, to help defray the cost of their education.

Considering Adolphe Monod's later reputation as a preacher, it is interesting to trace his early efforts in this area. As part of their curriculum, the students would prepare a sermon, sometimes spending months on it. Then they would deliver it at the seminary, where it would be critiqued by the professors. Later they might be asked to preach the sermon at a church in the area. Apparently, Adolphe's first attempt was not a success. One professor proclaimed, 'You will never be an orator!' Discouraged, he worked diligently to modify his effort before preaching it at a church in nearby Carouge. Billy gave the following account of Adolphe donned in the traditional robe:

> *He had a bit the air of a child, though a grave and serious child, well able to impose that seriousness on those older than he. Besides, everything harmonized in the service: small church, small preacher, small cantor, and even a small sermon. He was only elevated two steps above the congregation. [In larger churches, a small flight of stairs would lead to the preaching pulpit.] Nevertheless the whole*

time his expression was firm and assured. … The church was nearly full, and I believe they were generally edified and content. The sermon had more warmth than at the first recitation he gave in front of the professors. He had made a number of corrections.

Adolphe then laboured for months preparing his second sermon. This time his success was stunning. The students and professors at the seminary recognized in him a true gift of eloquence. In the summer of 1822, when Adolphe and Billy were in Paris for the wedding of their eldest sister Adèle to Édouard Babut, both young men were asked to preach, in succeeding weeks, at Sainte Marie, the smallest of the three reformed churches in Paris. Their father and many other family members were present, and the sermons seem to have been well received. This was when Jean first recognized Adolphe's great potential as a preacher. Fortunately, Jean had warned his son that a parade of Catholics — accompanied by drums! — might interrupt his sermon. The young preacher was advised to simply stop quietly until the parade had passed. This he did, with great calmness and poise, before resuming his sermon. He was slowly learning his craft.

Matters of faith

If the personal and academic adjustments to Geneva were fairly easy for Adolphe, the spiritual adjustment was not. Matters of faith that had seemed simple and clear within the confines of the family and of the Paris church became far less so in the atmosphere of seminary life. Cross-currents were everywhere.

The theology taught at the seminary was much like what Adolphe and Billy were used to — a respectful but tepid attitude towards the major doctrines, mysteries, and miracles of Scripture. They were not denied, but neither were they actively embraced and allowed to minister spiritual good to hungry souls. As Adolphe wrote:

> The pastors of Geneva occasionally talk about Jesus Christ from the pulpit — of the love we owe him, of his example, of his incomprehensible redemption — but it is more as a kind of concession to orthodoxy than as things that apply to themselves and that they want their listeners to apply. They seem to confess certain doctrines rather than sense them.

Alongside this familiar theology, Socinians, who deny the deity of Christ, were present on the faculty and among the city's pastors. Then there were more powerful influences from outside the seminary.

When Frédéric and his classmates arrived in Geneva, they encountered groups of Pietists, some of Moravian background, but the seminary did not permit its students to attend their services. Then a spiritual renewal swept into the city, building on some of the Pietist elements and emphasizing the Scriptures. God's primary agent in this movement was Robert Haldane, a Scottish layman and former officer in the British Marines who had abandoned his career to devote himself to evangelism. He was not a theologian, but he knew the Bible intimately. He arrived in Geneva in 1816, while Frédéric was a student, and for months he held private meetings with the seminarians, expounding the Epistle to the Romans. The effect of this book on the young men was akin to its effect on Martin Luther; their eyes were opened to the gospel. According to Frédéric:

> *Every circumstance seemed to be opposed to his mission of faith and love. … As for us, the young students, we were, for the most part, frivolous, filled with worldly thoughts, and immersed in earthly pleasures. Though we were students of theology, real theology was the thing we knew least. The Holy Word was for us an unknown land,* terra incognita. *…*

> *What astounded me more than anything else and gave me pause for reflection was his [Haldane's] practical knowledge of Scripture and his implicit faith in the divine authority of this Word, about which our professors were almost as ignorant as we. … We had never seen anything like it.*

Even given Frédéric's tendency towards seeing things in stark, black-and-white terms, this is a telling description. Many who were at Haldane's meetings were to become leaders of the powerful religious movement known as *le Réveil*, or the *Awakening*. Frédéric declared that through Haldane's ministry he had been 'begotten in Christ'.

By the time Adolphe and Billy arrived in 1820, both Robert Haldane and Frédéric had left Geneva, and the first wave of the Awakening had subsided. Yet a group of about 300 'dissidents' who had been touched by the movement remained in the region. This group, centred on the Gaussen family — relatives of the Monods — added to the mix of theological perspectives.

With differing views abounding, Adolphe soon found himself in a state of confusion that he later saw mirrored in his own seminary students.

> *As long as you lived, gently ignored, in the confines of the family home, the faith that you imbibed from infancy ... seemed to be so deeply rooted in you that no storm could ever shake it. ... Today you have entered far enough into the knowledge of the things of God to raise more than one embarrassing question, yet not far enough to resolve them. With fear, you sense thoughts of doubt ... insinuating themselves into your heart.*

Monod's confusion is seen in his constantly changing leanings, as they are revealed in his correspondence and diaries.

The most attractive of the groups was probably the dissidents, whom today would be called evangelicals but were then often termed 'orthodox'.

> *If you knew how I am drawn to orthodoxy. There is amongst these people a seriousness, a zeal, a devotion, a conviction that strikes me and makes me doubt my godliness. It makes me ashamed of my coldness and fearful of being in error. I want to leave aside all human consideration, take Scripture, my heart, and my conscience, and make a judgement. What good fortune that I am now occupied with the labour that can best prepare me to read Holy Scripture.*

(Note that he was not yet really studying the Bible!) Yet while he was attracted to the dissidents, he could not share their convictions. He even spoke of 'that pettiness of spirit found in some of our orthodox and ... that hardness and inflexibility that is found in others'. Their certainty on matters of doctrine both attracted Adolphe because it spoke of sincerity, and repelled him because the truths they espoused made no sense to his intellect. Still he sought out their company and frequently made visits to his cousin Louis Gaussen, who was then a pastor in Satigny, not far from Geneva. Gaussen, like Frédéric, had been a seminary student transformed by Haldane's ministry. Adolphe found Gaussen's sermons to be 'exaggerated', yet he wanted to hear them. He said to his cousin, 'One day I would like to believe more than I do, but less than you do.'

Then in 1823, another Scottish layman, Thomas Erskine, arrived in Geneva as a powerful witness for experiencing God's presence in a personal way. His theology was apparently relatively orthodox, yet it had a mystical or experiential element and lacked some of what Adolphe saw as the narrowness of the Gaussen circle. Yet this, too, failed to fully satisfy him. He wrote to his mother:

> While Billy was away, I made the acquaintance of Mr Erskine, who singularly interested and struck me. ... He caused me to see a number of things from a new point of view. His system is more ethical and philosophical than that of the Geneva orthodox. ... There is in him a zeal, a devotion that interests me. The result of this conversation will be to make me think. ... Beyond that it leaves me — or rather plunges me — deeper in my doubt and uncertainty on the subject of religious opinions. Orthodox, Methodist, Arian, I am each of these in turn. This uncertainty is a cruel but necessary evil,

*one from which I don't doubt that I can emerge in the end
with blessed fruit. In deciding right away, I would be at too
great a risk of making a mistake; by waiting, by reflecting
several years, I don't know whether I will find the truth, but
at least I will be closer to it.*

He could sense the power and truth in the Awakening,
he was drawn to the peace and assurance that it brought
to those who embraced it, but he wanted things to make
sense to his intellect, and they didn't. Perhaps the influence
of the enlightenment plus his own independence and
perfectionism hindered him from finding the peace he so
desired.

One result of his uncertainty was growing periods of
depression and self-doubt. These seemed to begin during
his second year in Geneva and progressed along with his
inner turmoil. He had met a problem that he couldn't master
with his will, intellect, and hard work. He had not yet met
and surrendered to God.

Thesis preparation

It was in this state of theological uncertainty that Adolphe
and his brother Billy began their last year of studies. It
was the autumn of 1823 and time for them to consider
the important task of writing their dissertations. Not
surprisingly, they chose related topics. Billy wrote on the
proofs of apostolic inspiration, Adolphe on the character
and extent of that inspiration. We don't know the state of
Billy's faith at this point, but Adolphe was feeling tentative.

'If I arrive at results that are too liberal, I will not publish in French; most assuredly, I will not publish. I do not wish to scandalize pious persons, perhaps only to retract my statements later. If I cannot settle my opinions on inspiration, I will openly say so and content myself with enunciating a few facts or theses.'

In the end, he did publish his thesis in French, under the title *Considerations on the Nature of the Inspiration of the Apostles*. Only a list of eight theses at the end was in Latin. Yet his opinions were clearly not 'settled'.

> *The Apostles of Jesus Christ were men inspired in their ministry; that is to say men miraculously enlightened and directed by God in the teaching, whether oral or written, of religious truth. I regard this fact as demonstrated.*

> *Once inspiration is admitted as fact, one can conceive of various opinions with regard to its nature. … Christians who agree in believing in the inspiration of the apostles can have very different ideas about it. This difference is so great that it is even the primary cause of all the divisions that are seen between them. The concept one has of inspiration determines the concept he has of the inspired books, and the concept one has of the inspired books determines the way in which he draws truth — which is divine thought — from them. …*

> *I would consider myself fortunate if I could indicate several clear and useful ideas on this subject. Yet to treat solidly and thoroughly a matter that is at once so important, so obscure, and so delicate would require a knowledge of*

Scripture that I have in no way acquired and insights that I do not possess.

Three things can enable us to judge the nature of inspiration: its goal, the descriptions of it we are given, and the effects that it clearly produced. From that, there are three questions that we propose for ourselves in succession:

1. What ought inspiration to be for God's desired goal to have been obtained?
2. How is inspiration described in the New Testament?
3. How is inspiration displayed in the lives and writings of the apostles?

Having laid out his three questions, the seminarian went on to devote a chapter to each. The shortest is the first chapter, where he concludes that 'in miraculously enlightening and directing the apostles, God desired to enable them to propagate the doctrine of Jesus Christ among men'. The other chapters are far more extensive, but he summed up his conclusions in the statement:

Inspiration was a general direction through which God, without constantly leading the heart and hands of the inspired men and without making them either perfect or infallible, furnished them successively, through means that were sometimes natural and sometimes miraculous, all the light and all the help necessary to establish Christian truth.

He acknowledged that these views would wound some, but argued that the importance of the subject required him to treat it candidly. 'May it please God that I never praise *the word of truth* at the expense of truth itself.'

The thesis already allows us to glimpse two qualities that were to characterize Adolphe Monod throughout the years of his successful ministry. First, we see a humility and openness about his ignorance, coupled with a hatred of hypocrisy. He is genuine. Second, we see him take a very logical approach to a thorny topic. At this stage in his life, the logic was still deeply rooted in his own reasoning powers. After his personal encounter with God, still three years away, such logic was tempered by a realization that there are mysteries related to the eternal realm that we cannot yet fathom while here on earth. This new consideration would lead him to focus on the practical side of theology.

Divine inspiration

Given Adolphe's thesis topic, it is interesting to see how his views on the divine inspiration of Scripture developed after he entered into a living faith. Here, for instance, is what he said about the nature of inspiration when he himself was a seminary professor drawing lessons from Jesus' temptation in the wilderness.

> *Are you puzzled about what theory of inspiration to adopt: what is its mode and extent, what part does it leave as man's contribution, does it direct the sacred author's spirit or his pen, and other questions of a similar nature? Here again, follow Jesus' example. On all of these speculative questions,*

he offers no explanation. But is it a matter of the practical question? Is it a matter of the confidence with which you can quote the Scriptures, all of the Scriptures, even down to a single phrase of the Scriptures? It is impossible to be clearer, firmer, or more positive than Jesus is. Go and do likewise. Quote the Scriptures as Jesus did, and have whatever theory you would like on inspiration.

Jesus has a vantage point more elevated and more disengaged from earthly influences than that of our theology. Let us follow him onto these heights where one breathes an atmosphere that is so pure and luminous, and where the haze with which earth obscures heavenly truth stops below our feet.

He took a similar approach to the proofs of divine inspiration, the subject of Billy's thesis, when, in 1852, he preached from 2 Timothy 3:16 on *Inspiration Proven by its Works.* He argued that, quite apart from any rational, logical arguments, just the Bible's superhuman utility 'for teaching, for reproof, for correction, and for training in righteousness' is itself evidence that its writers were divinely inspired.

This emphasis on the practical value of Scripture does not, however, mean that Monod never developed views on the nature of the inspiration and authority of God's Word. He did, but without losing sight of the element of mystery. He said in his *Farewells*:

[Scripture] is God's Word, true and eternal, and, at the same time, it is man's word where one senses the gleam of the human spirit and the beat of the human heart. It is

precisely in the moments where one best senses (in a Saint Paul or a Saint John, for example) the fight of faith and the persevering struggle against sin that one also senses best how divine is the light diffused into their souls. … That is why we can say that the Word is all the more divine for being more human. …

Scripture is the written Word of God just as Jesus Christ is the living Word of God. Those who rely on the human characteristics of Scripture to belittle its divinity use the same sort of reasoning as those who rely on the human personality of Jesus Christ in order to deny him the title of God. They fail to understand that human nature and divine nature are united in the person of Jesus Christ just as the human word and the divine word are united in the Scriptures. …

As to the way that the two natures fuse together in the one case and the two voices in the other, it is … a deep mystery, but, as Saint Paul tells us, 'the mystery of godliness'.

Ordination

Whoever else might have been offended by the views expressed in Adolphe Monod's thesis, the thesis was accepted by the faculty and by the company of Geneva pastors, which determined all religious matters in the city. Adolphe and Billy then passed a battery of exams, which were arduous, but which concerned them less than their dissertations. They were approved for ordination. However, they were also chastised for setting 'an unfortunate example of insubordination, especially through the ease with which we missed classes. These reproaches are a bit exaggerated, though it is true that we missed more than usual … Mr Vaucher accused us of "following the example of our brother Frédéric".'

Now Adolphe had to consider whether he was prepared to accept ordination to the gospel ministry. The previous October, perhaps in one of his depressed moods, he had written to his mother, 'If next July I am not more settled than at present, I will never be able to bring myself to take on the commitments and responsibilities of the ministry. No, it's impossible.' Now it was late June, and he found himself still unsettled as to the orientation of his faith, yet still drawn to his calling.

> Something that delights and encourages me is that I sense myself always more bound to this career, and each day I find myself happier for having embraced it. The same cares and anxieties that so often pursue me also make me congratulate myself for having embraced the state in which I will best be able to cure them and find the most lively, yet most tranquil and solid pleasures.

Both Adolphe and Billy were thus ordained and consecrated to the gospel ministry on 8 July 1824. Their father was ecstatic. A month earlier he had written to the brothers, 'Well, my good friends, here we are close to the moment when, should it please God, I will be with you to enjoy one of the sweetest joys heaven could add to those which it has already showered upon me through my children.' Then, after explaining the plans for his four-week stay in the Geneva area, he ends his letter on a whimsical note, 'The English and French governments are printing tables of logarithms in fifteen folio volumes. Do you want to subscribe?' Jean made the four-day journey from Paris to be present as two of his sons completed their examinations and were ordained to the Protestant ministry. The only two disappointments were that he could not take part in consecrating them and that his wife, Louise, could not be present.

Yet Louise was very much in their thoughts. As soon as the ceremonies ended, Adolphe took pen in hand to write to his faithful mother.

> Here we are; just a moment ago we became ministers. Before anything else, since we cannot have the pleasure of sharing this day with you, I need to tell you, my angel of a mother, the thoughts and feelings that occupy me. My father is here with us, we are very happy, and the only thing still lacking will be found again in Paris in a few weeks. As for me, I sense that I was wiser on this occasion than I typically am in times of religious solemnity or strong emotion.
>
> You know how I spoil these lovely moments through my scruples and anxiety. Even yesterday evening I experienced a feeling of fear and sadness at the thought of the approaching day. Yet the good advice I received, good reflection, a talk with my father — these restored me to a better disposition, thanks be to God. While the sense of my weakness makes me grave and serious, it doesn't make me sad. I hope, I believe, I know that since God has blessed our work and has visibly led us, right up to this entrance into our career, he will not abandon us at the most important moment of our lives.

Thus Adolphe Monod emerged from his years of seminary training with his once-firm theology in disarray but with a continued sense of his calling to the pastorate. He was twenty-two years old.

4

Crisis and victory

(1824–1827)

The question loomed large: What next? Adolphe and Billy may have accepted ordination, but they were not yet ready to assume pastoral responsibilities. The next two years were a kind of interlude for Adolphe, and it was at this time that his path began to diverge from Billy's.

Digging deeper

Following their ordination, a family friend, Mrs Gauthier, offered Billy the responsibility of being a companion for her son Étienne, who had a medical condition requiring someone always to be with him. Meanwhile, Adolphe turned down two possible employments, one as an assistant at a church in Amsterdam, the other as a tutor to two English boys living in Bonn, Germany. Instead he stayed in Paris, living in the family home near Montmartre. He continued his studies, led the family devotionals each morning, and did a little tutoring.

His studies included the Bible and books on theology, literature, and history. At first he tried working on sermons, but he soon discovered that, without a pressing need, he was making little progress and that it made his studies seem cold by comparison. The sermons were abandoned.

This pattern continued until May 1825, when Adolphe accompanied his father on a five-week visit to London. Jean was attending a meeting of the British and Foreign Bible Society, which had provided help for their French counterpart, and Adolphe went along to help his father with the English language. Though Adolphe's comprehension of spoken English proved to be somewhat weak, he managed to deliver a short speech for his father.

The trip to London also afforded them time to visit Adolphe's sister Adèle and her husband Édouard Babut. This brought Adolphe into contact with his friend Charles Scholl. A man of the Awakening and a strong evangelical, Scholl was the bachelor pastor of the French Protestant church in London and was taking his meals with the Babuts. He had already strongly influenced Adèle's faith. Then in late May, Adèle's only daughter, Louise, died of meningitis at seven months of age. Scholl's pastoral care helped sustain the grief-stricken mother, while the presence of her father and brother provided added support.

Adolphe's extensive conversations with Charles Scholl in London must have had a significant impact because at the end of his life, Scholl was one of the three people, along with Louis Gaussen and Thomas Erskine, whom he credited with being instrumental in bringing him to a vibrant Christian faith. Scholl's presentation of the gospel was practical, winsome, and wise.

In June, Adolphe and Jean returned to Paris, taking Adèle with them for a two-month visit to help her through the grieving process. Adolphe resumed his studies, delving into the Bible, yet he made little progress. In September, more than a year after his ordination, he wrote to a young friend,

> *Redemption keeps me busy and torments me. I don't know what to think about it. I have to believe that the apostles' expressions contain some fundamental truth that I have not yet grasped. ... Read the New Testament always in Greek, even when reading for your edification. ... At the moment, I am reading the Epistle to the Romans. What obscurity! ... The gospel, which often presents me with passages that astound me and sometimes wound my reason or feeling, has nothing that makes me despair more than this epistle. I read it, I reread it; I see nothing there, absolutely nothing.*

Thus while Adolphe continued to be drawn to people like Gaussen and Scholl, he was still relying solely on his reason and could make no spiritual headway. The Holy Spirit had not yet opened his eyes.

The need in Naples

Then the Paris routine was again interrupted. The doctors caring for Billy's young charge, Étienne Gauthier, advised a six-to-eight-month trip through Italy to benefit Étienne's health. The young man's mother had the idea of including

Adolphe on the trip. Adolphe was hesitant, but his parents, concerned that he was becoming too introspective, encouraged him to go. The brothers set out with Étienne Gauthier in October 1825, making several stops before settling in Rome for two months.

In addition to seeing the sights and absorbing the culture, Adolphe and Billy took turns leading worship services for the French-speaking Protestants who were there — about ten French and Swiss living in Rome plus thirty to forty visitors, mainly from Switzerland and Holland. For six weeks, the services were held in the chapel of the Prussian ambassador. One of the people they met in Rome was the sister-in-law of Thomas Erskine, the Scottish evangelical who had met with Adolphe in Geneva. Her faith, like Thomas', was deeply personal and made a strong impression on Adolphe. Finally, in mid-February the brothers and young Étienne Gauthier went on to Naples.

When they arrived in Naples, a port city on the Tyrrhenian Sea on Italy's western coast, they were surprised by how many French-speaking Protestants were there, with no church, no pastor, and no means of worship. Adolphe agreed to lead regular Sunday services, starting in mid-March. This was not as easy as it might sound. The government did not permit freedom of worship, so the services had to be held in a private home or in a foreign embassy with extraterritorial rights. The first services seem to have been held in the home of Mrs Palézieux Falconnet.

At this time, Adolphe was corresponding about his spiritual progress with Thomas Erskine. He had sent Erskine a copy of something he had written on biblical inspiration, perhaps

Bay of Naples with Mount Vesuvius

his seminary dissertation, and Erskine, predictably, wasn't happy with it. Adolphe took this in good spirit, saying it would cause him to look even more seriously into such an important question.

> This letter and the discussions I have had with you have had a real and very useful influence on me. It is not that they have led me to confess exactly the same theology and interpretation of Holy Scripture that you confessed, and you yourself would not want me to mould my theology on yours or on that of anyone else. Yet you have made me keenly aware of the necessity of seeking my beliefs where you have sought yours and to listen to the Bible instead of judging it. You made me see that I have only a very superficial belief in Holy Scripture, that I have not yet felt the gospel, that religion has not yet changed me or even truly touched me. …

> I would give a lot to have several more conversations with you. I hope the occasion will present itself and that time will strengthen the relationship I have begun with you.

He was beginning to get glimmers of where the solution to his spiritual malaise might lie, but he was still far removed from experiencing it, and the desired conversations with Erskine were not to occur for over a year.

A crisis develops

In the meantime, the French-speaking Protestants in Naples urged Adolphe to become their interim pastor. He agreed, but only for one year, hoping that this would relieve his spiritual confusion. Instead, his confusion soon escalated into a crisis.

The birth of the small church was aided by the Prussians. They provided their embassy chapel as a more permanent place of worship and found a German-speaking pastor to work with Adolphe in ministering to the Protestant community. They even appointed a governing body or consistory for the new congregation and arranged for a salary for both pastors. Yet Adolphe needed more than practical help; he needed spiritual help, especially as it soon became clear that the German pastor really only wanted to preach one sermon a month in German. All the rest of the pastoral duties fell to Monod.

There he was, a young man of twenty-four with no pastoral experience, no firm conviction as to his beliefs, and faced with responsibilities for which he felt (and probably was) inadequate. To make matters worse, loneliness set in after Billy and young Étienne left in early May. He was by himself in a foreign city, away from the friends and family who could have encouraged and supported him. They did what they could through correspondence and prayer, yet still he felt alone. Adolphe's friends in the congregation were looking to him for spiritual guidance; he could not go to them with his problems. What was he to preach? What was he to teach his catechism students? This is when the melancholy that had begun in seminary became more acute. His correspondence indicates a mood fluctuating between hope of resolving his spiritual crisis and despair of doing so.

The young pastor's changing moods and shifting spiritual perspective make the next fifteen months a difficult period to understand. His inner turmoil is evident, but what was God's overarching trajectory for his young servant? Jean Monod expressed the opinion that Adolphe's faith was stronger than he thought it was, and this may be correct. Except for very brief periods, Adolphe didn't doubt that the truth he was seeking lay within the bounds of Christianity and the pages of the Bible. However, he had not yet found his place within those bounds, nor had he found an interpretation of Scripture with which he was comfortable. He didn't seriously doubt his calling to the ministry, though at times he was tempted to leave it, at least temporarily.

Perhaps the most important issue during this season of Adolphe Monod's life was a struggle to find the right balance between heart and mind, between feeling and reason. On the one hand, as a child of the Enlightenment era, he wanted to figure things out and to have them 'make sense'. On the other hand, he was drawn to the warmth and assurance of faith he saw in Thomas Erskine, Louis Gaussen, and Charles Scholl, yet he was afraid to let go and embrace it until it satisfied his intellect. He wanted to accept Scripture's teaching, as they did, but he also wanted to judge it. He still needed to find a place of humility and dependence before God. The wonderful balance and harmony between head and heart that emerged at the end of his inner conflict was one of the great strengths of his ministry for the remainder of his life, and there were forces that did not want to see that balance struck, but God was using this time of crisis to prepare his chosen instrument to spread the truths of the Awakening.

A ship at sea

At this crucial juncture, Adolphe's father tried to offer practical wisdom, advising his son not to rely solely on improvisation (preaching from an outline) but to take the time to compose some of his sermons carefully. This was totally impractical, given the other pastoral responsibilities weighing on him. Jean also responded to Adolphe's negative views of Naples by encouraging him to focus his efforts, not on the lukewarm Protestants, but on those who were truly rejoicing to see worship being established in the city. Jean hoped that others would be drawn in over time. Yet the senior Monod could not really understand his son's malaise. 'I am not disturbed very much by those doubts on which you seem to place more importance than they have, first because you exaggerate them and are more believing than you think, and then because, while envying the happiness of those to whom all seems clear and certain [i.e., the evangelicals like Erskine and Gaussen], one cannot help but see too complete a sacrifice of their intelligence.' Jean Monod had not been touched by the Awakening, and he was unwittingly stirring up his son's intellectual pride and thus feeding the very conflict that Adolphe needed to resolve.

This inner conflict spilled over into Adolphe's pastoral concerns. As his own spiritual doubts remained unresolved, he began to wonder how he could lead his congregation and whether he should leave his position as soon as his one-year obligation ended. Or perhaps sooner. He was torn between his own innate candour and a genuine concern for his flock. His father had advised him to leave Naples, but Adolphe also sought the advice of his cousin Louis Gaussen.

In August 1826, three months after Billy's departure, he wrote:

> *Your friendship for me and your perfect faithfulness to the cause of the gospel make me seek your advice on a question that greatly relates to my happiness and that could relate to the advancement of God's reign in a city that is Christian in name but almost pagan among its Catholics and unbelieving among its Protestants. ... I have never been a good Christian, still less a faithful minister, yet neither was I unfaithful enough to refuse a post that God's hand seemed to offer me. So here I am, a pastor in Naples and committed for one year. ...*

> *I thought I saw God's hand, the assurance of his help, and the beginning of my conversion to reason and godliness ... but alas, quite the contrary to what I hoped has happened. My inexperience, my ignorance, the weakness of my faith, conversations with the unbelieving ... and, above all, my native mental anxiety have all shaken my faith. ... I have reflected as to what I should do. On the one hand, I clearly*

cannot leave the new-born church without a pastor, but on the other, by remaining at my post I would do harm and not good to the souls God has confided to me if I shared my doubts and opinions with them rather than preaching the gospel. Therefore I take the course — painful to my candour but necessary — of preaching what the gospel teaches without considering whether I believe it or not.

I thought this decision was the end of my anxieties. I was wrong … I had fallen from unbelief of the mind to that of the heart. … I know that I have a will, that God rejects none of those who want to come to him. I know that, but I don't believe it, I don't feel it. …

In this situation, what should I do? Should I continue my stay beyond my commitment, as will be proposed and as is now being proposed? Should I leave at the expiration of my commitment? Should I leave before then and have a successor by this autumn, if possible? … I recall that a Moravian said to Wesley, 'Preach justification by faith before having believed it and you will soon preach it because you have believed it.' He found this to be good counsel. Should I not also preach the gospel before believing it, and will it not happen that I will then preach it because I have believed it?

Adolphe Monod might not yet have believed the gospel, but that didn't stop God from using the young pastor's labours. The little church was filling a real need in the city. Eight months after his arrival in Naples, the worship services were regularly drawing seventy to eighty members of the city's Protestant community, which numbered only about 130, including the Germans.

In the end, Adolphe remained at his post, at least in part because he didn't know what else to do. He couldn't accept another pastoral position or teach at a seminary in his current state of spiritual doubt; nor did he want to return to his parents' home and live off their support with no employment and nothing to occupy his time.

A sister's faith

If Adolphe's father could not fully comprehend his struggles, his sister Adèle Babut in London could. Her letters to him during this period bear eloquent testimony to the depth of her faith, the closeness of her relationship with her brother, and her insight into his problems. In May 1825, her infant daughter and only child, Louise, had died. Then in February 1827, when Adolphe had been in Naples for a year, Adèle lost a second daughter, about six months old. Three days later, she wrote a remarkable letter to her brother.

> *She is no more, my dear Adolphe; at least she is no more for us in this world, this beloved little Marie, source of so many consolations, joys, and hopes. Sometimes it seemed to me that my Louise had been given back to me; now I seem to have lost her a second time. Dear Adolphe, how wrenching is the agony through which I have just passed once again! How painful is the void left by the loss of a being so tenderly loved and who already was giving so much happiness! …*

> *Adolphe, in this solemn moment, I thought also of you. No doubt it was God who, in his infinite goodness, said to my torn soul that it could also receive blessing on your*

behalf and that the anguish of your poor sister could be the source of the Christian peace that we ask for you with such fervour. Dear Adolphe, if I am not mistaken, if my daughter in her death could preach to you with more eloquence and conviction than all those who have been seeking your good, ah, how true it would be to say that the day of her death has greater value than the day of her birth. I would thank God for all I have suffered. The thought of the happiness of my daughters and of the happy change in my dear Adolphe would alone remain in my heart and would give me the strength to resign myself to all that may still await me, convinced that no sorrow would be too much to pay for such a great benefit. …

Oh, in these days of misery and mourning, what would I become without him! If he is not alive, if his words are not eternally true, where can we draw strength against so many sorrows? But may he be blessed for the conviction he places in my soul. Oh, may he deign to make it pass into yours as well!

Adolphe, dear Adolphe, give him your heart. Love him for the good that he does for me, while waiting to love him for the good he will do for you, once you come to him with humility and simplicity of heart. Do not seek to understand him; you will understand him enough once you have learned to love him. And how could you not be grateful for his mercy towards me, you who have always been so tenderly attached to me!

Her last advice, 'Do not seek to understand him', shows how well Adèle understood her brother. That is just what he was trying to do. Adolphe wrote to his mother, 'I received Adèle's letter. I have no words for the admiration she inspires in me. This is the ultimate in charity! How fortunate she is! How fortunate! I will, no doubt, answer her tomorrow or Thursday, but what will I say to her? Oh, my God, courage! I will tell her the truth, such as it is in my heart.'

Seeking a way out

This crucial and wrenching season in Adolphe's life also contains an amusing but telling anecdote. One Saturday evening, he apparently decided to follow his father's advice for combating his sadness: 'get out, take a walk, go see something'. He ventured out to a party with dancing. A young girl asked with amusement, 'Are you here to prepare your sermon for tomorrow, sir?' Adolphe was pierced to the heart by such mocking and immediately left the party, resolving never to set foot in a ball again. Worldly distractions were not the way out of his spiritual dilemma.

Given his spiritual crisis and the fact that the period of his initial commitment was coming to an end, Adolphe Monod again began to think about leaving Naples. The obstacle was finding someone to replace him as the Protestant pastor. He made inquiries in Paris and Geneva, and the candidate who emerged was Louis Vallette, a friend from seminary days. Adolphe was hesitant about Vallette's preaching ability, but in April 1827, after Adolphe's initial commitment to the Naples church had already ended, Prof. Cellérier from the seminary recommended Vallette highly. Vallette applied for the position, and the consistory and congregation in Naples rapidly voted to accept him as their new pastor. Relieved, Adolphe thought he saw an imminent release from his painful obligations. He was wrong. Vallette declared that he could not come before November. Monod begged him to come by the end of June, but Vallette responded that 1 October was the earliest possible date for his arrival in Naples. The Lord had more work to do in Adolphe Monod before he left his post.

A visit from Thomas Erskine

Near the height of this crisis, Thomas Erskine visited Italy. Arriving in Naples in May 1827, he spent several hours a day talking with Adolphe, sometimes in Erskine's room, sometimes as they travelled by foot or carriage in the country. At first Erskine talked about his own faith and tried to answer Monod's objections, encouraging him to pray and read Scripture.

> As to Holy Scripture in particular, I gained a desire, for perhaps the first time in my life, to know it well. As Mr Erskine has only a few days left in Naples, I begged him to use them to read the most difficult parts with me, and I wanted to begin with the Epistle to the Romans. We are reading it in Greek. ... After that we will read the Epistle to the Hebrews. ... It would be difficult for me to give an account of the effect that these readings and conversations have had on me. My thoughts are too troubled for me to see them clearly. For the moment they [the conversations] have troubled my peace.

The young pastor's faith continued to waver; he spent much time in introspection, and his mood and resolve were changeable. Still the overall effect of Erskine's visit was positive. Adolphe Monod's reactions were recorded in his journal.

Tuesday 15 May to Monday 21 May:

My conversations with Erskine have convinced me of my need for something that I have not yet found and that I cannot give to myself.

I sense and I see in Mr Erskine and in others a happiness, a peace, an order, a conviction that I totally lack. … I am in a state of disorder and sin. I sense it; I am out of harmony with myself; my philosophical principle is unsatisfied. The creature's perfection can consist only in his relationship with the Creator; yet — and this is my sin — I have been my own centre until this very moment. … I wanted to make my own religion, instead of taking it from God. … Only an external influence can save me.

Conclusion from conversations with Mr Erskine:

God of truth, you cannot refuse me truth! You are committed to make me find it. You are committed to it by the promises of the Gospel! You are committed to it for the sake of my catechism students and of my sheep. You are committed to it by the sacrifice you have obligated me to take on and by the prolongation of this sacrifice. … That is why I am resting on you. Because my only remaining uncertainty regards the moment when you will be pleased to enlighten me, I want to hasten that moment by henceforth acting as if certain to find the truth. I will seek it in the place where I have most reason to believe it will be found, in the Bible and in those who have faithfully explained the Bible. ... Give to my body and mind the necessary strength to work, to think, to seek you, and to find you.

Here we see glimmers of the needed humility and dependence, but they were just transient glimmers. By 25 May he was becoming wary of too much reliance on feelings. He wrote to his parents:

Mr Erskine is in Sorrento for several days. I am relieved. ... I was letting myself be drawn along too much by him. ... He judges by feeling and proves things through imagination. His book is a series of comparisons that are not always tied together well, and besides, comparisons are not reason. I, on the contrary, have had enough of feelings. I like only that which is clear and exact, and I would like to be busy with mathematics or the natural sciences, not philosophy and religion.

As the letter proceeds, it reveals two major stumbling blocks that Adolphe Monod could not overcome. The first is salvation by grace through Christ's atonement for our sins. 'These ideas do not speak at all to my heart.' The second is man's free will and his inherent sinfulness. 'Who will explain to me how man is endowed with *a free will*, in such a way that all corruption is voluntary and punishable, and yet this free will *cannot* will good, so that we can be sure in advance that all men who will come into the world will be sinners?'

Safe harbour

Shortly after this, he despaired and decided to give up his spiritual quest. His goal was to study Italian history and the Italian language, but after a week he abandoned that and resolved to give the best hours of the day to reading the Bible, studying theology, and preparing his sermons. By 17 June, he thought he could see some progress. He was beginning to read Scripture with a more open mind, 'taking its meaning rather than giving it mine. I pray with little fervour but a bit of confidence'. Eight days later, he was praying in agony, 'Have pity on me! … Give me what I lack. What is it? I don't know, but you know. And if, in order to receive it, I need a certain disposition of mind, give me that disposition too. I can do nothing for myself.' Adolphe Monod was, at last, reaching the end of himself.

Finally on 21 July 1827, weeks after Erskine had left Naples, the crisis ended. It isn't clear what, on an earthly plane, finally wrought the dramatic change he had sought for so long, but God's time had arrived. Real peace came into his life. He left his lodging in the morning and was walking through the streets of Naples, when he was overcome with sorrow, almost to the point of shedding tears. Then he said to himself, 'Others before me have been just as sad. They found peace in the gospel. Why shouldn't you find it there?' He hurried home, fell on his knees and let his despair burst forth in a torrent of weeping, pouring out his heart to God. Until the end of his life, he always regarded this as the day of his conversion. Twenty-eight years later, during his last illness, he recounted his experiences to a young friend in need of what he had received.

From this day on, a new inner life began for me. Not that my melancholy disappeared, but it lost its edge. Hope had entered my heart, and since I have been engaged on this path, the God of Jesus Christ, whom I had just learned to trust, has done the rest, little by little. ...

You can believe me, my good friend. It was not new arguments or having objections resolved that gave me this helpful direction. Rather, sensing at the bottom of my heart that I was helplessly miserable, I threw myself, without reasoning or reserve, into the arms of a God of love, whom the gospel revealed to me.

This was a dramatic and long-sought change, and at first he was hesitant to trust that it would endure. As his confidence grew, he began to write to those dear family members who had supported him with their prayers, comfort, and counsel. He wrote first to his parents, then to Billy, and finally to his faithful sister Adèle.

Glad tidings

Adolphe and Billy had shared their lives to an unusual degree until Billy and Étienne Gauthier left Naples to continue their travels. It is not clear how or when during the intervening fourteen months Billy arrived at a deep, evangelical faith, but apparently he did. Now the two brothers were one in an entirely new way. Adolphe wrote to Billy:

You say that you want to speak to me of nothing but the gospel because nothing else interests you any more. Very well! Me, too! I will thus treat the same subject. ...

Ever since Saturday 21 July ... I have not stopped praying and reading the gospel with confidence. Without being exactly happy, except perhaps in hope, I have not had one moment of melancholy in these nine days ... The ease with which I passed from unbelief to faith in several days or even in one day is a clear proof to me of God's work in me. ...

Did you read commentaries in order to be converted? I have no desire to do so. I would rather hold to the Bible — to the gospel and the psalms that is — and to the little book Mr Erskine left me, which is doing me so much good. Is it laziness that distances me from commentaries? I don't know. Yet I fear that if I threw myself into them before being established in the faith, I would grow weary and cold. I am so weak! In the end, I ask God to make his will known to me in this regard as in all others. May his will alone be constantly and perfectly accomplished in me.

A couple of weeks later, he wrote to Adèle.

My tender and beloved Adèle, you are a sister who has pushed fraternal love and Christian charity towards me to the point of finding consolation in the death of her only child. If God used the rending of her heart to restore peace to mine, such a sister has first rights to be told immediately of the first steps God has caused me to take in Christian peace. That is why, my tender and beloved sister, having waited only the time necessary to assure myself that what is happening in me is not a working of my natural capriciousness but an operation of the One in whom there is no shadow of turning,

I come to give you the best of news about me. ...

In reading the gospel, I forgot that I could neither understand nor receive it unless God himself prepared my spirit. ... Then, seeing as if by a shaft of light that my spirit was and always had been in a state of blindness and wandering that had to cease if I were to have peace ... and seeing that I thus had no hope save in an external influence, I remembered the promise of the Holy Spirit. Learning in the end through necessity that of which the positive statements of the gospel had been unable to persuade me, for the first time in my life I believed in that promise in the only way it could best speak to the needs of my soul. I believed in it as a real, external, supernatural action ... exerted over me by a God who is the master of my heart as truly as he is the master of nature. ... Renouncing all merit, all strength, all personal resource, and recognizing in myself no claim on his mercy other than my misery, I asked him for his Spirit in order to change mine.

As we saw, this is the perspective he still retained at the end of his life. His reason had gone from the role of master — the arbiter of truth and judge of Scripture — to that of a servant of the Holy Spirit and a student of Scripture. He still had questions, and he knew he needed to grow in his faith, but he was prepared to wait, knowing that he would find the answers he sought in the pages of the Bible. He had encountered God, and the new inner life he began that day eventually solidified his doctrine and transformed his preaching.

5

Testing by fire

(1828–1832)

Adolphe Monod's new faith was soon to be tested, but not in Naples. After his conversion, he considered staying on there but decided against it. His friend Louis Vallette had promised to come and relieve him by 1 October 1827, so Monod's young congregation was cared for. Vallette turned out to be a faithful and devoted pastor for the Protestants of Naples, remaining there for fourteen years. Yet his predecessor never lost his affection for his first congregation or for the friends he had made in the city. He kept in touch through his correspondence with Vallette.

Once relieved of his responsibility for the Protestant church in Naples, Adolphe Monod returned to Paris for a brief visit to his family, before being invited to Lyon. The consistory of the Reformed Church of Lyon was interested in hiring him to fill a vacancy on their pastoral staff. They had noticed his talent for preaching and knew that he was from an esteemed family of ministers. He preached a trial sermon on 28 October 1827, just three months after his conversion, and immediately afterwards the consistory voted to hire him. He began his duties in December, shortly before Christmas. He was not quite twenty-six years of age.

Temple du Change in Lyon

The church in Lyon

This was a very different situation from Naples, where the Protestant community was extremely small and there was no established church. The city of Lyon was a large commercial centre at the confluence of the Saône and Rhône rivers, in one of France's prime wine-growing regions. Because of its strategic location, it had once been the capital of the Roman province of Gaul. The main centre of Protestant worship was the Temple du Change, located just off the Saône River in the heart of the old city. It had been built in the mid-seventeenth century as the Loge du Change, or stock and money exchange, and was enlarged a century later. It was abandoned after the French revolution, and was unused until 1803, when the government assigned it as a worship centre for the French Reformed Church. The area around Lyon had about 10,000 Protestants, mostly inside the city, yet the Temple du Change could seat only 600. Shortly before Monod's arrival, the national government had granted permission to hold services in two additional locations in the nearby towns of Tarare and Sainte-Consorce. Some of the Lyon congregants, including members of the consistory, were prominent businessmen and merchants who were influential in politics and social life.

The Reformed Church of France, as we saw earlier, was authorized under the Organic Articles of 1802, which required the French government to approve the hiring and dismissal of pastors, pay the pastors' salaries, and appoint the members of the local consistories. The consistory members were typically chosen more for their wealth and prominence than for their spiritual qualifications — a practice that led to great theological diversity.

The consistory in Lyon was one of the most worldly, and its members would not have hired Monod if they had recognized the new nature of his theology. But they didn't. At the time of his candidature, his 'religious ideas' were 'not yet fixed', so his trial sermon failed to alert them. It is also likely that the candidate failed to discern the nature of the ruling body over which he was soon to preside. This ignorance on both sides would not last long.

The Monod family and the Awakening

As Adolphe Monod was launching out on this new phase of his life and ministry, it is worth considering the spiritual evolution of his family members. Three of Jean and Louise's sons had already been ordained for gospel ministry, and all three — Frédéric, Billy, and Adolphe — had been touched by the Awakening and come to a strong evangelical faith. We also know that Adèle's faith had likewise taken on new life and vibrancy. Interestingly, Jean and Louise had quite different responses to these developments — developments which eventually spread to include all of their 'twelve sparrows'.

Jean, a pastor himself, was deeply concerned that the faith of his sons had taken on an 'extreme orthodoxy', and he had apparently expressed this concern to them. This troubled Adolphe, who was still processing his own conversion and settling his beliefs. In later years, Jean was proud of his sons' successes in ministry but never comfortable with their theology. He wanted to draw them back to the cold, formal piety they had grown up with, even as they hoped to see him embrace the warm vitality of the evangelical faith. As one contemporary put it, 'They claimed to be new men, and he had remained the same.'

Louise, on the other hand, had no professional stake in theology. As a perceptive woman, she could see the positive difference in her children, and the warmth of their newly awakened faith made her realize the coldness of her own. Having encouraged and prayed for Adolphe during his time of spiritual crisis, she was now in a spiritual crisis of her own. Shortly after Adolphe arrived in Lyon and just four days after Christmas, she wrote him a touching letter.

> *You were happily inspired in giving the sermon of preparation [for communion] that gave us so much pleasure. I would truly like to hear it from your lips today, as I get ready to take communion with a soul that is, alas, ill prepared to do so. I suffer from sadness and discouragement at the thought of my unworthiness, at the thought of how my time is spent, the way my whole life has been spent. What great need I have of the grace and mercy of my God!*

> *I do not despair, but I astonish myself in daring to count on that grace when I think of my coldness, my ingratitude, and my distractions throughout this long life. Life for me has been so filled with blessings of every type and help of every kind, yet it has been so empty of love for God, of confidence in my Saviour, of charity, and of good works! May I at least not approach the sacred Table unworthily! It is painful to me never to go with the joy that should characterize every true Christian. Pray for me, my cherished son. I count much on the prayers of my children. More fortunate than I, they will not have waited until the end of their course to think of giving their hearts to God.*

Adolphe and her other children must certainly have prayed for Louise. Though her spiritual struggles, like Adolphe's, went on for years, we know that by the end of her life, she had acquired a like-minded faith.

In the meantime, Frédéric was serving with his father on the pastoral staff in Paris, Billy would shortly become a pastor in Saint-Quentin, and Adolphe was adjusting to his new position in Lyon. All three congregations were part of the French Reformed Church.

Beginnings

When Adolphe Monod arrived in Lyon, he was one of two pastors and served under Gustave Pache, a considerably older man who planned soon to retire. In searching for Pache's replacement, the consistory at first tried to hire a senior person, but when he withdrew his candidacy, the consistory voted in January to hire Joseph Martin, the young man who had been the other candidate for Monod's position. Pache retired in June 1828, just six months after Adolphe Monod's arrival. Thus Monod — age twenty-six, newly converted, and with little ministerial experience — became the senior pastor of a large congregation. Martin arrived in the city a month later, in July.

At first Adolphe Monod was well received and invited into many homes, where he became acquainted with his parishioners. Some, including a number of prominent and influential women, were of evangelical faith. One of these was Mrs Évesque, whose husband was the deputy mayor of

Lyon and served on the consistory. Yet the prevailing view within the congregation, including its elders, was liberal Protestantism.

Through Mrs Évesque, Adolphe Monod met Baroness Pelet de la Lozère from Paris, herself a devout Christian. She and some of her female friends, both Protestant and Roman Catholic, had organized the Paris Bible Society, whose mission was to make the Bible available to everyone, rich or poor, whatever their religious background. This group frequently sought Monod's advice, and he took a sincere interest in their work, hoping to see it replicated in Lyon. Mrs Évesque remained a friend and supporter of Adolphe Monod all through his stay in Lyon. Likewise Baroness Pelet and her husband were to play important roles in Adolphe's life and in the development of his career.

Not all the pastor's time was taken up with the wealthy and prominent. As his doctrine began to solidify and his preaching began increasingly to reflect his new-found faith, Adolphe Monod began to bring a greater measure of unity to Lyon's Protestant community. A group of evangelicals, mostly humble folk, had previously left the French Reformed Church and were holding their own worship services. Once the direction of Monod's preaching became clear, their leader came to him in warm friendship and said he was giving up those services and would find it a joy to be among the young pastor's listeners.

Yet there were signs of trouble. While the dissidents were pleased with Monod's preaching, most of the consistory members definitely were not. Monod later wrote:

The consistory at first treated me with singular good will and esteem that its subsequent actions have in no way caused me to forget. … It had been only a short time since my spirit had been opened to the understanding of Scripture and I had recognized the truth of the doctrine that is called orthodox. …

It was not until February 1828 [two months after his arrival] that I clearly expounded the way of salvation for the first time in a pair of sermons … Man's Misery and God's Mercy. Since then, my preaching, following the development of my personal convictions, has become ever clearer and more characterized by the meaning of Scripture and of the Confession of Faith. I could tell that from that time it began to displease certain people and worry the consistory.

Adolphe was also beginning to experience loneliness. While he was invited to various homes, there was nobody with whom he was close enough to just drop in on when he felt in need of company. The family that might have filled that role was the Honymans. Mrs Honyman was a widow of Scottish origin living with two grown children: a daughter Hannah and a son William. Monod felt comfortable with them, yet he was fearful of visiting them too often. He didn't want to burden a family with few financial resources or be accused of favouring foreigners or start rumours that he was courting Hannah. His mood brightened a bit as he prepared to move into the apartment at the Temple du Change that Pache was vacating, especially after Billy arrived to help him make the transition.

Adolphe Monod's duties were not too burdensome while Pache was still the senior minister. Adolphe took his turn preaching in the main services, did regular hospital visitation several times a week, and perhaps taught catechism classes for those preparing for communion, but he was spared the many administrative jobs that fell to him after he became the head pastor and president of the consistory. As senior pastor, he also took over leading the short daily worship at the two Protestant schools in Lyon, one for boys and one for girls, plus a weekly evening Bible service at the church.

The young minister was ill-prepared for so much responsibility, especially since his faith was still so new, and the stress of all Pache's former duties probably contributed to his health problems. He complained of serious stomach pains, perhaps due to ulcers. In September, with Joseph Martin on the staff, he asked for a leave of absence to recover his health. This was granted and then extended when he did not immediately improve. He returned to Lyon in late January 1829.

Rising opposition

It was during Monod's four-month absence that the consistory first began to work towards getting him to change or resign. They also hired a young assistant pastor, Eugène Buisson, who, like Martin, leaned towards liberal theology.

In spite of stress and opposition, Monod continued to preach what he believed, and as his convictions developed, his sermons increasingly displayed a prophet's zeal. Before his leave of absence, he had preached *Sanctification through the Truth*, arguing biblically that no one can be sanctified — that is, can learn to love God and desire his will — without knowing the truth. Sincerity in one's convictions is not enough. This was followed early in 1829 by *Sanctification through Free Salvation*. Salvation by grace and the need for personal repentance were new concepts to most of his congregants. They expected to earn their salvation through good works. Nor were they used to thinking of themselves as sinners, whether saved by grace or not, and they found the idea offensive. They were children of the Enlightenment.

Then on Easter 1829 Monod asked the probing question, *Can You Die in Peace?* A long sermon in its published form, it systematically, mercilessly, but biblically demolishes all its listeners' false hopes for a favourable judgement at their death based either on their own conduct or on a softening of God's standards. Then, at last, Monod holds out to them the reason for his own assurance, the only true reason for assurance: the 'one mediator between God and man, the man Christ Jesus' (1 Timothy 2:5). His hope, their hope, our hope lies only in the cross of Christ and in his having paid the penalty for our sins. This was completely contrary to the prevailing view and even to the congregation's funeral liturgy (which the consistory refused to modify).

Monod was displaying youthful zeal and impatience. His own spiritual struggles had lasted for years, yet he seemed to expect his parishioners to readily embrace the teaching of the Awakening, which now seemed so clear to him and which he tried so carefully and forcefully to explain.

And so the problems between Adolphe Monod and the consistory in Lyon continued to escalate. As Monod's sermons got more forceful, the consistory took stronger and stronger measures to get him to leave. This, in turn, only made him more anxious to preach the gospel. He would not back down on what he knew to be true. He wrote to Louis Vallette, his friend and successor in Naples:

I returned from my leave last January [1829]. On 14 February, I asked the consistory's authorization to hire an assistant at my own expense. Agreed, but I had to choose one and submit my choice to the consistory. On April … 24th, I proposed an assistant to the consistory. He was turned down as well as any other who would share my principles. *I thus resigned myself to being alone.*

17 May, I preached on Romans 6:1 and showed that far from being hindered by faith, not one single good work is possible in a soul that has not believed in free salvation through Jesus Christ. This sermon was more displeasing than the other [his Easter sermon].

On 30 May, the consistory met to decide on sending me a delegation to invite me to change my preaching and my conduct. I received them on 2 June, and having invited them to explain the kind of change they desired — which was that I should preach and act as if I did not believe in free salvation — *I replied that I could not do so. On 5 June, the consistory ruled that my presence in the church was doing harm, and they asked for my resignation, but not until I had been given the hearing I requested. I was heard on 20 June and showed first that they had no cause to ask for my resignation unless there was proof that I was not fulfilling the duty of my ministry. This I invited them to prove. Second, I answered the complaints that had been brought against*

> *me. Some I acknowledged to be well grounded, promising*
> *to profit from them; others I showed to be unjust. On the*
> *25th, the consistory asked in writing for my resignation while*
> *making no reference to my remarks, which they could not*
> *refute. On 1 July, I refused to resign, also in writing, and left*
> *for Paris the same day.*

He planned to see his parents and then go on to visit Billy in Saint-Quentin.

Hannah, the end of loneliness

One of the purposes of the trip to Paris was to consult his parents about a possible marriage to Hannah Honyman. Their growing relationship was a rare happy development during this period of rising conflict with the consistory. In the years since completing seminary, he had often considered the possibility of marriage, but he had never found the right young woman. Now he saw in Hannah just the qualities he was seeking.

Hannah Monod

The Honyman family — father, mother, three daughters, and a son — had moved to Lyon following the fall of Napoleon in 1815. The father, John

Honyman, passed away in 1823, followed by a daughter Mary in 1825 and another daughter Margaret early in 1828. Adolphe Monod was introduced to the family by a mutual friend at around the time of Margaret's death, when they were in need of pastoral care.

While Adolphe had felt comfortable with the Honymans, he had hesitated to spend very much time with them. In the summer of 1828, he briefly considered taking an apartment in the house where they lived and was, perhaps, considering Hannah as a potential marriage partner (as rumours suggested), but his parents advised against it because of the tuberculosis in her family.

In the spring of 1829, after Adolphe returned from his leave of absence, Hannah's brother William developed the disease. With this new need for pastoral care, Adolphe was soon making daily visits to the family, which brought him into frequent contact with Hannah. With a growing attraction, Adolphe sought the advice of physicians as to whether she was at risk of tuberculosis. Assured that she was not, he decided to rent the apartment below the Honymans' and to take his meals with them, informing his parents that he wanted very much to marry Hannah. Not long after that, Hannah's brother died.

The two concerns that Jean and Louise had about a marriage to Hannah were her health and whether the young couple would have sufficient financial resources. Adolphe had reassured them about Hannah's health, but their monetary concerns remained. Both Jean Monod and Adolphe's grandfather, Gaspard-Joël Monod, had married women from wealthy families, which relieved them of financial concerns, at least in the early years of marriage. Jean and Louise seem to have wanted the same benefit for their son. However, when Adolphe assured them that he and Hannah could manage, his parents realized that his mind was made up and left the decision to him. In late July, Louise wrote:

> *Every day I become more settled in the opinion that you alone should decide your future. You will find no further opposition from us. If, on the one hand, this union doesn't offer all that we would have desired to find for you, on the other, it demonstrates a precious harmony of sentiments and views. It will remove you from your isolation, which could have gone on indefinitely and become very troublesome to your morale and your health. I am not without concern for your financial position. …*
>
> *Hannah's little letter is charming. I assure you that I love her and that I sincerely desire that God will be pleased to remove all obstacles so that you may marry this woman who is so much after your own heart. … Farewell, dear children.*

Two weeks before the wedding, Adolphe expressed his happy confidence in the marriage in the same letter to Louis Vallette that told of the consistory's opposition.

> *I write to communicate first to you and then, through you, to my former parishioners … the news of my upcoming marriage. I am marrying an English woman [Hannah was born in London, though her family was from Scotland] who has been resident in Lyon for some years. Miss Honyman is a Christian, born to Christian parents, raised by them in*

the faith from childhood, mature in experience both in the world and in the gospel. She is two years older than I am (I am almost twenty-eight), gifted through nature with great abilities and much useful knowledge, and gifted through grace in God's most precious gifts: an enlightened, deep, sweet, and humble godliness. I paint this picture for you because, knowing me well, you will realize that she has exactly what you would doubtless most desire in a wife for me.

I have the sweet conviction that in combining the rather different gifts that we have each received in our characters, we will, between the two of us, make one good and useful minister of Jesus Christ. Moreover, my joy and hope lean on something more solid than the evaluation I make of her; they rest on the full and deeply grounded conviction that, having both walked by prayer for a long time, we have been led by God, who has caused us to see that he himself chose us for one another. This gives us the certain hope of his most precious blessings on our union.

Now the young couple faced a delicate question. They deeply desired to be married by a minister who shared their evangelical faith. This meant bypassing the expected choices of either Jean Monod, who would be making a trip to Geneva and could detour through Lyon, or Adolphe's colleague, Joseph Martin. In the end, they invited a friend, César Bonifas, to come from Grenoble to conduct the ceremony, though Martin was asked to serve as a witness. The marriage took place on 2 September 1829, with no members of Adolphe's family present.

The choice of Bonifas to perform the wedding created further friction with the consistory, and the fact that no members of Adolphe's family were there grieved his parents. Jean visited the newlyweds almost two months after the wedding as he was returning from Geneva to Paris. He was pleased with Hannah but was not invited to preach, as would have been customary. Adolphe's new religious convictions were adding strain to family relations, even as they enriched his personal life.

The newlyweds had a short honeymoon before returning to face Monod's escalating difficulties with the consistory. He was going to need the understanding support of his new wife.

The heat of conflict

Even during the wedding preparations, the consistory persisted in its efforts to force Monod to leave his post. His letter to Vallette continues:

> I returned to Lyon last week, August 10 [from the visit to Paris and Saint-Quentin]. In my absence, the consistory had removed my catechism students and invited M. [Joseph Martin] to instruct them, not just until my return but until their first communion. Beyond that, the consistory wrote to my father asking him to solicit my resignation, but I did not think it proper to sacrifice what I believe to be God's will to my father's influence any more than to the consistory's authority, so this method also failed. They have only one thing left to do: they must call for my dismissal by the

government. But being unable to allege anything against me except my principles, they will not succeed.

So that is where we are. It is, in one sense, a sad position, but in another a happy one, in that this very opposition proves that the Lord has allowed me to touch a wound, that the church in Lyon is not completely dead, and that it is beginning to come back to life. People have been converted since my arrival in Lyon, some of them through my ministry. We have some fervent and mature Christians, and we are waiting on God for great blessings on this church.

Those were the facts, and the situation was, at best, awkward for the young pastor as he embarked on married life. His faith was solid and in accord with the doctrinal standards of the Reformed Church of France, but he was also humble enough, even in his zeal, to have some inkling that he was contributing to the problem. The letter goes on:

Am I somewhat at fault? Perhaps my liveliness and energy have sometimes passed the limits of gentleness in my preaching, especially when preaching extemporaneously, as I almost always do. Perhaps something too stubborn or austere in my voice and mannerisms — my miseries, in short — have contributed to this irritation. Yet that part is very small. The main cause for the opposition, almost the only cause, is the clarity and boldness with which the Lord enables me to proclaim salvation through the cross, which seems madness to my listeners, almost all of whom are worldly.

His preaching reflected a sense of urgency. He didn't know how long any of his listeners might continue to live, and he carried a burden for their souls. And so the fire of his preaching continued to grow, leading him eventually to address the social ills that were tied to the spiritual ills.

His 1830 sermon *Are you a Murderer?* posed a number of probing questions. For instance, 'In your workshops, have you abused the needs of the poor and the weakness of childhood to burden them with excessive labour, causing them to vegetate, languish, grow pale, and slowly die for the sake of your well-being and pride?' Yet the intent of such questions was to point his congregants to their need for a Saviour, whose love and mercy he always held out to them. Acknowledging his own need, he said, 'If there is somebody here who resembles me; if there is someone here who recognizes himself, perhaps for the first time in his life, to be bad, condemned, lost, cursed by God, let him rejoice. It is specifically for him that the voice came down from heaven, the voice that comes forth again from every page of the Bible: "Grace! Grace! Grace for the criminal; salvation for the one who is lost; eternal life, the kingdom of Jesus Christ for the one who is on the pathway of eternal death and in the kingdom of Satan."'

The balance may have been too much on the side of recognizing sin, yet ultimately it was his theology — the theology of the Awakening — that was the real problem. It was alleged that he had come to Lyon 'to seriously compromise the divine calm that we were enjoying', and that 'the loveliest, the most difficult, the holiest of all religions will always be *the religion of good works*'. False rumours were spread (he saw visions of angels; he was in the pay of the British), and petitions calling for his resignation were circulated from house to house. This was a lot for a young man to endure, yet he did so without rancour or bitterness.

Fire from the pulpit

The final, decisive issue was communion. The consistory already knew of Monod's distress that the congregation did not adhere to the confessional standards on admission to the Lord's Supper. He had issued increasingly forceful pleas, urging members to examine their faith and their lives before coming to the Lord's Table, but little had changed. Then, on 20 March 1831, preaching from an outline, he spoke with unusual passion.

> *Where am I? Is this truly Christ's Church? Is this truly the Reformed Church of France? … Will communion days always be days of mourning, scandal, and anguish for a faithful minister? As for me, I would rather place the body of Christ on a stone and throw the blood of Christ to the winds than deliver them into an unbelieving and profane mouth. … This is pure unbelief, unbelief clothed in the name of Christ, so that in the Church of Jesus Christ, under the name of Jesus Christ, perhaps even in the pulpit of Jesus Christ, in those who are established to watch over the sheep of Jesus Christ, there, even there the demon has placed his unbelief! This is no longer Christ's church; … it is the assembly of Satan!*

According to one description, 'Never was his eloquence raised to such a level of force and holy passion. His burning improvisation thundered like a storm.' Youthful zeal and the opposition he faced seem inadequate to explain such extreme rhetoric, but years later, when the sermon was republished, Monod hinted in its preface that extraordinary situations had existed in the congregation. Presumably he knew of specific instances of grossly inappropriate and blatantly sinful behaviour by one or more prominent members who went uncensored.

The consistory was outraged by this sermon. At their meeting on 14 April, Monod presented a proposition for the re-establishment of scriptural discipline surrounding the Lord's Table. Rather than approving it, they used it as further grounds to ask for his removal. On 15 April, the consistory voted to petition the government to dismiss Adolphe Monod from his position in Lyon. In their petition, they accused him of wanting 'to re-establish a kind of inquisition, which, though sanctioned by Church Discipline, fell into disuse centuries ago'. Beyond that, the elders knew he was scheduled to preach *and serve communion* on Pentecost, and they hoped to have a new offence to add to their petition if he failed in his duty to administer the sacrament. The beleaguered pastor went to his Master in earnest, agonizing prayer.

> *My God, you know that I cannot serve communion on Sunday in this confusion. I thank you that you have made this point clear to me, and you will clarify the others as well. Oh, show me now how I should carry out what you have commanded. Grant me, Lord, a clear sense of your will.*

Having sought unsuccessfully for someone to preach in his place, he simply delivered his sermon and left the building prior to the distribution of the elements. The result was that the consistory voted to suspend him from all formal ministry functions, pending the government's decision on his case. He continued to receive his government salary but not the consistory's supplement, which had been discontinued the previous year. Finances were tight. Yet still Monod was careful not to let bitterness towards the consistory or his parishioners invade his heart.

The aftermath

The government's decision did not come for many months, and although Monod by this time expected it to go against him, he felt no liberty to pursue other employment until the matter was settled. In June 1831, he made a visit to Paris and preached a number of times. It was a joy to be with his large family, most of whom he had not seen in two years. Returning to Lyon, he exercised what ministry he could.

> *I am strengthened in the thought that the substance of my life should be used for the active functions of the pastorate: going from place to place in Lyon, exhorting, converting, consoling, praying, explaining the Word, whether among the unconverted who would like to hear me or among the children of God. The remaining time should be given to necessary reading and the composition of a few articles.*

One important ministry had begun before his suspension. The previous year, he had started holding informal gatherings to explain the Scriptures. The consistory had forbidden him the use of the Temple du Change, so the meetings were held in Adolphe and Hannah's home. In spite of the fact that

Monod had not been allowed to announce these sessions from the pulpit, there was an average attendance of eighty to a hundred persons prior to his suspension, and presumably afterwards as well.

During this period of waiting and uncertainty, Adolphe Monod also had time to think and pray about what he should do if the government approved his dismissal. His situation was well known and keenly watched among French-speaking Protestants, and his services were being solicited. A new school of theology had been formed by the Evangelical Society of Geneva, and they wanted him to join their faculty. In addition, two groups of dissident Christians in Lyon were looking to him. One group had left the national church and formed a small, independent church late in 1830 as Monod's troubles with the consistory were escalating. They still had no pastor, so in October 1831, they voted unanimously to ask Monod to take on this position. The other group comprised Christians who had continued to attend the national church until Monod's suspension and who were now frequenting the informal Sunday services in his home. Neither group had access to the sacraments. Monod, as an ordained minister, could have celebrated them in the gatherings in his home, but he wanted to avoid any appearance of willingly separating from the national church.

In January 1832, Adolphe got word through his friend Mrs Évesque (wife of the consistory member who was deputy mayor of Lyon) that his dismissal had been approved. The royal decree making the decision official was issued on 19 March 1832, signed by King Louis-Philippe, but the beleaguered pastor did not receive written notice until 10

April, a year after the consistory voted to fire him. Nearly four years of growing tension and strife had ended. This was the first time the government had approved dismissing a pastor without specifying a cause — a precedent that disturbed evangelicals all across France. It seemed to give the local consistories the ability to fire pastors without cause.

In evaluating Adolphe's difficulties in Lyon, it is worth noting that Billy was having similar problems in Saint-Quentin. The two brothers, so inseparable in their early years and now united in their faith, were both finding opposition to their preaching. When Adolphe had visited Billy in July 1829, the consistory in Saint-Quentin had already expressed their displeasure with Billy's sermons, and Adolphe's efforts at mediation failed. Soon afterwards the consistory asked for Billy's resignation, which Billy refused to give. Considering the different temperaments of the two brothers, the parallel development of their relations with their church elders suggests, as Adolphe believed, that the main problem in Lyon was not Adolphe's zeal, boldness, and lack of tact, but his theology. Billy, too, was eventually dismissed from his post, though with the added cause that he developed a serious mental illness. He eventually recovered and was able to return to the pastorate.

Why did Adolphe Monod endure so much unpleasantness and resist so much pressure to resign? It was because his preaching and conduct were in accord with the Bible and the 1559 *Confession of La Rochelle*. He thus felt compelled to remain where God had placed him and to proclaim the truth. Many did not like his message, but they needed to hear it.

6

Breaking new ground

(1832–1836)

The verdict had been delivered. Adolphe Monod's association with the Reformed Church of Lyon had ended. Now he was faced with two crucial decisions: Should he publish his explanation of his conflict with the consistory, as some urged him to do? And what ministry did the Lord intend for him to pursue? He had had months to consider these questions; now it was time to decide.

Looking back

Should he publish? With all evangelical eyes in France watching Adolphe Monod's conflict with the consistory in Lyon and with that conflict having reached its conclusion, should his fellow Christians be given an explanation of what really occurred? It would be tempting for a young man to

Lyon from the Rhône River

want to justify himself, but would that not simply prolong a painful conflict and aggravate wounds that needed to heal?

In 1831, after the consistory petitioned the government to confirm their dismissal of Monod, the Minister of Public Instruction and Worship invited the young pastor to present his side of the issues in writing. Monod framed his memorial to answer the specific charges brought against him, but his explanations were drawn from a larger and differently organized discussion of what transpired. Now some evangelicals were urging him to publish that discussion. As always when important issues were at stake, Monod went to the Lord in prayer and sought godly advice. Two days after receiving formal notice of the decree, he wrote to his brother Frédéric.

> As to publication, I have seriously considered it for a fortnight, yet I always have a distaste for the work. ... Nevertheless, I believed it to be necessary and timely. I

have consulted Gonthier [François Gonthier, a godly and respected Swiss pastor who had just spent two days visiting Lyon]. ... Contrary to my expectation, he expressed the definite opinion that this publication ... would only produce irritation ... would distance from me persons who are perhaps open to be drawn in (wives and family of members of the consistory), and would necessarily have much of a personal nature. Given those considerations, it should be pursued only based on a perfectly clear manifestation of God's will, which did not seem to him to exist up to this point. ... His intentions ... seemed to me to be in accord with wisdom, patience, and charity. I have submitted to them. ... For my part, I am weary of fighting, but I am at the Master's disposal.

The reference to 'wives and family of members of the consistory' would certainly include Mrs Évesque. This godly woman continued to support and encourage Adolphe Monod's ministry and to offer wise counsel.

Thus Adolphe Monod's discussion of the issues surrounding his dismissal was laid aside and preserved for another thirty-two years. In 1864, eight years after his death, his family published the account, just as he had written it. They had felt the necessity to wait, as they said, for 'the deep sense of a service rendered to the cause of truth, the conviction of a faithful duty to be fulfilled. This moment of serious necessity, foreseen by Mr Monod himself has now arrived'.

Here again, one is struck by all lack of bitterness in Monod's heart. The boldness and zeal of his preaching were not indicative of personal animosity against the lay elders of the church but only of deep spiritual convictions and a sense of urgency in drawing his parishioners to Christ. His zeal was for the Lord and for the gospel.

Moving forward

The question of Adolphe Monod's future ministry was also resolved by prayer and godly counsel. He received two job offers from Switzerland. The new Geneva School of Theology renewed their invitation for him to join their faculty, and an evangelical church in Lausanne wanted him as their preacher. Both offers were attractive, especially the first because of his love for Geneva, his long-standing interest in seminary teaching, and the chance to work with his cousin and dear friend, Louis Gaussen. Both offers would also have provided a salary adequate to support Monod's growing family. Yet in the end, he rejected both and stayed in Lyon with no guarantee of financial support. He felt an ongoing pastoral responsibility to the Christians there, just as he had earlier felt a responsibility to those in Naples. His brother Frédéric, after meeting with other evangelicals in Paris, had encouraged this decision.

> We were unanimous in thinking that you cannot leave Lyon right now. The task at hand is to establish a faithful church. Afterwards, God will show you if he wants to call you elsewhere. ... None is positioned as you are today to establish that church, and the Christians of Lyon must not be abandoned. It is of great importance to show the consistories that if they can drive pastors out of the national

church, they cannot drive the gospel out of those places where it has begun to be preached.

There was great concern that the situation in Lyon would be replicated in other cities across France, so Adolphe would be setting an important precedent in founding an independent, evangelical church.

Adolphe Monod's own thinking on the subject was expressed in a long letter to the Evangelical Society of Geneva, turning down their seminary post.

The prayer we have together offered to God … that he would show me his will so clearly that I could not be mistaken in it has been answered with his usual faithfulness.

[Monod then describes the two groups of Christians in Lyon in need of a pastor.] The eyes of both groups are looking towards me. They have been waiting for me, and my deliverance [from ties to the Reformed Church of Lyon] seemed as if it should be their deliverance as well. During this waiting period, we have all got to know each other better and better, and the universal desire is to form one single body. As I have the confidence of both groups, I am looked upon by all as called of God to bring about the desired union.

The decision was made. Adolphe Monod would stay in Lyon, not to become the pastor of the dissident church but to incorporate its members into a new church that would have its own unique characteristics.

The task of establishing the young church was not easy. Most of his parishoners were fairly poor, and they came from varying church backgrounds. What they shared was having been touched by the Awakening. They had encountered God personally and desired to follow him faithfully. In addition to the Christians, people who were not yet believers were attending the Sunday evening Bible expositions. The young pastor sensed the magnitude of the task and his need for divine guidance.

> *14 April — Lord, make the way straight before me! I have consulted with brothers, and I could not find light. My soul was troubled. Now, my Saviour and my God, you who have given me this work to do, it is you alone I want to consult. … Enlighten me even today, if possible, Lord. …*
>
> *Lord, I need to act in such a way that the work of Lyon might serve as a model for all the other churches of France that might find themselves in the same position. I need to walk slowly, taking only one step after another and not taking a single one until I am assured of having the Lord with me.*

A question of authority

As the groups came together in 1832 to form one body in Christ, one of the biggest potential problems was church polity. This was noted even in the dissidents' letter asking Monod to become their pastor.

> *While we know that your views on church government are different from ours, this did not cause us a moment's*

hesitation in making our request of you. We are convinced
that this divergence will be lost in love.

The issue was that Adolphe Monod, true to his Huguenot heritage, still had great respect and love for the Reformed Church of France and its doctrinal standards. Thus he wanted to maintain the general practices of the national church, but without control from the secular government. He insisted on infant baptism, and he wanted the pastor — and eventually the elders — to control most things, including access to the communion table. The dissidents, who were from a congregational background, wanted adult baptism and a more democratic form of governance. These issues were, indeed, eventually 'lost in love', but the process was not always easy.

In early June, Adolphe Monod wrote out his principles for guiding the nascent church.

I would like, above all, to found the new church on principles
… that are scriptural, simple, charitable, and broad. They
should be suitable for the growth of the Christian life, not
merely in word but in deed. The principles that God has
caused me to understand on this matter must be those
that prevail. I cannot yield on this point; I can only follow
the simple and straightforward course that comes from
my position as a dismissed pastor, departing as little as
possible from the usages of the national church. … Yet, at
the same time, I would like to broaden my awareness, put
the separatists at ease, calm minds, etc.

This was a fine line to tread. He was also sensitive to the fact that his position was an exception to a general rule.

That which elsewhere would be a spirit of domination was here a positive calling which I could not avoid without compromising the work. ... In a word, this was not a fully established church calling a pastor and telling him, 'These are our principles.' This was a pastor designated by circumstances to found a church, calling Christians to himself, and telling them, 'Here are my principles. Let those who share them follow me.'

He didn't really want all that responsibility and looked forward to a time when he could share it with others. After deacons were chosen and Monod had hired an assistant, the pastors and deacons formed a governing council that functioned much like the consistories in the national church.

The sacraments

One of Adolphe Monod's first priorities was to re-establish the sacraments. He had stopped celebrating them after his suspension from the Reformed Church of Lyon. Now he felt free to administer them again.

With regard to communion, he still sensed the keen need to limit access to the table. Only those who had truly accepted salvation by grace through Christ's sacrifice on the cross and whose conduct did not contradict their confession should be admitted. He also regarded it as his pastoral duty to decide who met those criteria. Thus on 20 April, Good Friday, just ten days after official notification of his dismissal, he announced to the new congregation that he planned to serve communion one week after Easter and that those who wished to partake should meet with him to be approved. The object of those private conversations was 'not to rule the conscience, still less to replace it, but to direct it, enlighten it, lead it gently, and thus to let it choose its pathway — and choose it well — through a clear vision of its own state compared with the positive declarations of God's Word'. Twenty-five men and thirty women were approved and participated in the Lord's Supper; fifteen more were asked to wait.

That first communion service was the official launching of the new congregation. 'This was a beautiful day, and I don't know if my ministry had ever been sweeter. It was beautiful through the ceremony itself, a communion of God's children communing in spirit and in truth. It was beautiful through love, since gathered there before God and men were Lyon's Christians, being lifted up by brotherly love above the nuances of position that had previously separated them. It was lovely through their number'. The regular schedule at this time was a Sunday noon service for preaching, a Sunday evening service for Bible exposition, and a Saturday evening prayer meeting.

But all was not yet harmonious. When Adolphe announced the next communion service for Pentecost (17 June 1832), the leader of the congregationalists asked that members have a voice in who should be admitted to the Lord's Table. Monod still felt he should decide, and he did so for the June service. After several more months of prayer and consultation, this became the rule of the church, in spite of some lingering opposition.

Baptism was addressed next and proved to be a more thorny issue. Adolphe and Hannah had a one-year-old daughter named Mary who had not been baptized because she was born just a few days before Adolphe was suspended by the national church. Mary's parents were anxious to remedy this situation. The dissidents, however, felt strongly that baptism should be restricted to those who had come to saving faith in Christ. When Adolphe announced at the 13 May preaching service that he planned to baptize Mary the following Sunday, the leaders of the dissidents complained. They did not even want to be present for an infant baptism. The issue was resolved by performing the baptism after the close of the regular service, so those who desired to do so could leave. This became the regular practice in the church.

Early growth and organization

By early June, the services were clearly outgrowing the pastor's private residence. Monod, therefore, arranged to rent a hall at Maison Thiaffait to serve as their chapel beginning on 1 July. The hall was located on the Rue de la Vieille Monnaie, a busy street in the centre of Lyon, near the confluence of the Saône and Rhône Rivers. With a seating capacity of two to three hundred, it provided important room for growth. In addition, space had been rented for a free Protestant school for boys.

In August 1832, Monod launched a Sunday school, and the schedule was changed. The preaching service was at 10.00am, Sunday school at 3.00pm, and Bible exposition at 6.30pm. That was a lot of church for one day, yet the pastor felt that the Sunday school was important because there was not yet a school for girls during the week.

Also in August, the church was well enough launched that Monod felt he should begin to call congregational meetings every two weeks. The discussions were to avoid a controversial spirit, and women were not allowed to speak or vote.

Finally Adolphe Monod decided to hold monthly meetings on missions and monthly 'Question Meetings' where members could ask theological or doctrinal questions. These were addressed in a general discussion that Monod only led and tried to steer in directions of 'general usefulness'.

All this was accomplished within five months. The Evangelical Church of Lyon was taking shape rapidly. As Monod wrote, 'God was walking ahead of us. All our wisdom was in following him, and he showed us, step by step, what we should do. … It is a good thing for man to wait on the Lord and to follow him. And how much more is this needful in establishing a church! The more it is a work of faith, the more it needs to be a work of patience.'

Reaching out

The new little church continued to attract people, sometimes because of its location, sometimes by the witness of its members, but always by the Lord's faithfulness in drawing others to himself.

Some come first out of curiosity and later return with better feelings. Women have come to the chapel, have got Bibles and, not knowing how to read, have had them read to them by their husbands, who were then led to accompany them to hear the preaching. ...

One of our brothers found himself in a barber shop. He began to talk to the barber about the gospel, but he didn't seem to be listening. However, a stranger who was present heard, took the address of the chapel, and came with his whole family. ...

A mother and daughter who were subject to the priests ... refused the Bible for a long time. Finally the mother agreed to accept a New Testament. ... After reading it for just a few days, she found pleasure in it and shortly afterwards also wanted to come to the chapel. One Saturday evening, the day before she counted on coming for the first time, her daughter, in despair that her mother was going to be won over, created quite a scene, with pleas and sobs, hoping to dissuade her, yet without being able to shake her. Sunday morning she said, 'Very well, mother, since you are absolutely determined to go to the chapel, I will go with you, in order not to leave you, but you will go to mass with me.' They came to the chapel and were both won over. They forgot the mass, and ever since have been diligently following the preaching, loving the Christians, and reading the Word of God with interest, faith, and delight.

The question meetings were also blessed by God, who used them to attract people to the worship services.

These simple discussions have served not only to enlighten and strengthen souls already well disposed [towards the gospel], but to awaken many persons from their unbelief. Among the questions being presented, we have had the great satisfaction of hearing more than once the question of the Philippian jailer, 'What must I do to be saved?' ... In these same meetings, we have sometimes also met with painful discussions, yet they served, by God's grace, to set the truth in evidence. These are sometimes raised by Roman Catholics but more often by unbelievers.

Then, in October, the Evangelical Society of Geneva sent colporteurs to go through the district selling inexpensive Bibles and New Testaments. When they found a particularly promising reception in an area, they would alert Monod, who would go and preach there. This led to the formation of little outposts of the gospel, each with a small number of serious persons continuing to learn and grow in the faith.

By the time of the Christmas communion service, thirty new people were applying to be admitted to the Lord's Table in Lyon itself; two-thirds were from a Catholic background. The number was large enough that Monod instituted what was basically a catechism class, though many who attended were at least forty years old, not adolescents. Towards the end of the church's first year of existence, there were 100 to 150 in attendance at the morning service and 150 to 200 in the evening.

Paying the bills

Even with growth, finances were a problem. Most of the members were poor silk workers, so the church relied on gifts from outside. Their pastor was relying on God.

> He gave me such a clear view of his leading in what was happening to us, such a firm conviction that our work was prepared and sanctioned by him, that I undertook it without finding in Lyon anywhere near the funds to meet our needs. By faith, I took on obligations for the chapel, the school, etc., following the principle that we should not spend even one unnecessary penny but that we should also not doubt that the money for all essential expenses would arrive. My expectation was in no case disappointed.

Indeed, the Lord provided for their initial needs in amazing ways that left no doubt as to his agency in the situation. He was building the faith of the members of this fledgling church, even as he was strengthening the faith of their pastor.

> I had not even completed arrangements for the chapel when a Christian lady from England from whom I had not solicited help and whom I knew only by name told me that if I needed money, she would send me fifty pounds sterling (1250 francs). [The church's budget for the year was between nine and ten thousand francs.] Afterwards, a Christian from the same country whose name I learned only through his first letter, placed at my disposal 150 pounds sterling (3750 francs), payable over the course of one year. Just after we named our deacon, the same person sent several hundred francs

destined for our poor. About the same time, a Christian from France gave us a gift of 900 francs.

These gifts show not only the Lord's faithfulness, but also the international interest in the work.

Even so, contributions covered only about two-thirds of the first-year's costs, and these represented only the most needful expenditures. The church was forced to accept two loans, one from an American friend. Meanwhile, the pastor's family showed ingenuity in finding ways to reduce their living expenses to the barest minimum. In later years it was wonderful to look back at the Lord's provision, but in walking through those days, there were many anxious moments.

As the congregation launched into its second year, Adolphe Monod met with a group of evangelical pastors and laymen in Paris, describing both the Lord's past provision and their future needs. The group was enthusiastic and sympathetic, contributing 4700 francs themselves and appointing a committee to help raise additional funds for Monod's work. At their suggestion, he wrote a booklet entitled *Appeal to the Christians of France and abroad on behalf of the Evangelical Church of Lyon*. It was published in April 1833 and was apparently distributed by the committee with the names of agents in Lyon, Geneva, Lausanne, London, New York, Boston, and Hartford through whom contributions could be made.

His *Appeal* gave a detailed account of the church's first year and laid out the needs for the coming year. But 'our greatest need, dear brothers, that which you should ask of God for us — and, alas, is it not everywhere the thing most lacking for God's children — is love — love for God and love for the brothers. Lord, increase our faith, but above all increase our love!'

The success of the *Appeal* is hard to assess, but a letter in late 1833 mentions two gifts: one for nearly 800 francs from a gentleman in New York who had read the booklet, the other for 600 francs from someone in the south of France.

Plombières-les-Bains

All this activity took its toll on Adolphe Monod's health. His earlier stomach difficulties recurred and again required him to take a leave from his pastoral duties. In early July 1833 he left for a six-week trip to Plombières-les-Bains to seek relief. Plombières is a hot-springs resort located in the narrow valley of the Augronne River in the upper Saône region, north of Lyon. The trip was a time of rest and healing but not a time of inactivity.

On arriving in Plombières, Monod located a few evangelical Christians who were also staying there. He immediately began to hold Sunday worship with the believers and to meet with a smaller number for fellowship each evening.

The Christians staying in Plombières joined Monod in distributing tracts in the region. One Saturday, they decided to journey by donkey to nearby Vallée des Roches (Valley of the Rocks). At the last minute, the donkey masters went

Vallée des Roches

back on their word, but arrangements were soon made to hire a canvas-covered cart drawn by two oxen. The voyagers sat on hay bales, perhaps reminding Monod of his boyhood excursions when he and his siblings rode in a cart perched on top of bales of cotton. The trip took about four hours, suggesting that they stopped to distribute tracts. When they arrived at Vallée des Roches, they found 'huge rocks hanging on either side of the route and covered by lovely forests of fir trees'. Awed by the beauty and majesty of the fir trees, reaching heavenward to a height of seventy to eighty feet, the weary travellers ate a picnic lunch on some grass, with the oxen grazing contentedly beside them. Then they took a different route back to Plombières, arriving in a mere two hours. 'On the way back, we had an interesting conversation on the means by which a Christian may attain real holiness and a regular sense of God's presence.'

Adolphe Monod's congregation in Lyon was not forgotten during his time in Plombières. Correspondence and prayer kept them on his heart. 'How to draw the church out of her inner listlessness and outward inactivity? ... I feel we are suffocating and in need of fresh air. ... I don't know what to do. I would prefer, if possible, to draw the world's attention and respect through highly eloquent preaching, highly distinguished schools, excellent organization, and the radiant holiness of the Christians. ... But this would be quite slow.'

Unfortunately, when Adolphe returned to Lyon, his health was not much improved, and he was obliged to take his family — now consisting of Hannah and two daughters — to a place in the country nearby for about another six weeks. On returning once again to Lyon, he hired an assistant to help carry out his ministerial duties. Even so, the press of obligations continued to tell on his health. Again in the summers of 1834 and 1835, he needed to seek the healing waters and peace of Plombières. In early September 1835 he wrote in his journal,

> Peace. *I have learned to give a bit of my burden over to the Lord. ... This can only be done through a complete renouncement of self — self-glory as well as self-will. Psalm 131. This perfect abandon can be reconciled with the use of active measures, but such reconciliation is not easy. It is necessary, or I will be crushed. There is no possible peace for me except in unburdening myself in this way onto the Lord.*

A difficult but needful lesson was being learned.

Sermons and ministry

Back in Lyon, a large part of Adolphe Monod's ministry was always his preaching. In a sermon simply entitled *Creation*, he highlights our total dependence on divine grace by drawing a number of analogies between God's creation of the world and God's creation of a new heart in a believer. Another sermon, *Omnipotent Faith*, used the Canaanite woman as an example of the kind of persevering, prevailing faith that God seeks in his people. These are reminiscent in tone of his early messages in the Reformed Church of Lyon, yet we begin to hear more of the Adolphe Monod who was later to be called 'the voice of the Awakening'.

In May 1834, he was invited to give a pair of discourses in Mens for the consecration of two men to the pastoral ministry in the Reformed Church of France. The structure of these sermons, *God's Compassion for the Unconverted Christian*, is reminiscent of the earlier pair *Man's Misery and God's Mercy,* preached in Naples and revised for the Reformed Church in Lyon, but the focus is narrowed to nominal Christians. Though their tone is fairly strong, these sermons reflect Monod's life-long burden to see spiritual vitality restored to the national church.

There were several other threads to Adolphe Monod's ministry at this time. Evangelism among Roman Catholics continued, and the church began to reach out to English and German Protestants in the city. After his first trip to Plombières, he also began to participate regularly in the *Correspondance Fraternelle*, an exchange of letters between evangelical pastors on subjects relating to their ministries. In October, he wrote about a pastor's responsibilities, including praying for church members individually and preaching with feeling. The following January, he dealt with the relative merits of writing out sermons and preaching from an outline. Family correspondence shows him addressing his mother's continuing spiritual struggles and offering advice to his youngest sister, Betsy, regarding her Christian walk. Other surviving letters offer counsel and encouragement to acquaintances who had contacted him. His pastoral heart was broad.

An enduring hymn

While Adolphe Monod's sermons are too long to be studied here in detail, some of the same characteristics appear in a hymn he wrote in 1833 for a new hymnal entitled *Chants Chrétiens*, or *Christian Songs*. The book was published the following year, with a second edition appearing in 1837. Hymns were not generally used in the French Reformed Church at the time, so the desire to produce this book most likely reflects the growing influence of the Awakening and, perhaps, the emergence of independent, evangelical congregations.

The theme Monod chose shows the dramatic change wrought by his conversion. In Naples he was prone to periods of melancholy; now he recounts the happiness or blessing or joy that a Christian can know. The same theme recurs in a sermon he gave a few years later called *The Happiness of the Christian Life*. The hymn has seven verses.

1. *Oh my Saviour and Lord, dear God, what yet can I do*
   To fill all earth and heaven with your goodness divine?
   I ask them to proclaim my highest praises for you
   And tell the whole world o'er the joy that now is mine!

2. *There is joy when I hear and know your holy Word.*
   It said 'Let light shine forth', and the light then obeyed.
   It stoops to teach my heart from all that I have heard
   And says, 'Here is the path by which you may be saved.'

3. *There is joy when I speak to you from earthly dust*
   And let my praise and vows to the heavens ascend,
   With freedom as a son before his father, in trust;
   A sinner who has fear for God who has no end.

4. *There is joy that your day — the day that saw there arise*
   Your work from out of nothing and your Son from the
       grave —
   Will lead me to the courts where saints are offering
       praise,
   Rekindling all my zeal that now is prone to fade.

5. *There is joy 'neath the blows that fall from your faithful*
       rod.
   I'm punished but in love and in love suffer pain.
   I weep, yet with no doubt of the Father-love in God;
   I weep beneath the cross; I weep, but not in vain.

6. *There is joy when attacked by the messenger of Satan.*
   My weapon is the cross and my Saviour the Lamb.
   I triumph on my knees, and when the enemy's beaten,
   I find myself with wounds, with victory in hand.

> 7. *There is joy, ever joy! The Father is my God,*
>   *Christ Jesus is my Saviour, and the Spirit my guide!*
>   *What now can hell remove, what's left for earth to add*
>   *For those who love our God and in his courts abide?*

This English adaptation preserves Monod's rhyming scheme and uses the term joy, which seems best to capture his meaning. The word 'joy' here is not necessarily a bubbly, effervescent joy, particularly in view of verses 5 and 6. Rather it can be a deep, quiet, peaceful joy arising from our knowledge that all the circumstances of our lives are ordered by a loving, all-powerful God. It is joy in the Lord, a joy that only a true Christian can know. Monod experienced such joy, even during the intense suffering that marked the end of his earthly life.

The hymn's content and structure are quintessential Monod. As in his preaching, he uses the repetition of a phrase (in this case, 'There is joy...') to mark the structure of his work. It is also characteristic not to gloss over the harder aspects of the Christian life, while always putting them in the perspective of the cross and of what the Christian gains. Even the ordering of the verses is significant. Most of us would have put the verses about being punished (5) and suffering demonic attack (6) ahead of the verse on being called to heaven (4). Yet apparently Monod wanted to remind worshippers of their eternal destiny so as to give them a better perspective on the more painful seasons we encounter. This is a bit like his three sermons on *Jesus Tempted in the Wilderness*, where the second sermon builds our confidence of gaining victory in our battle, before the third describes our weapon, the Word of God, and how we are to use it.

Monod's hymn soon took its place among the classics — a hymn 'that all Protestants know by heart'. Various melodies were used, though the version given here is best suited to *Éternelle Splendeur*, written by Ami Bost (1790–1874), a strong evangelical and an acquaintance of Monod. The hymn was eventually included in other collections of worship songs, and several anthologies of French poetry, where it was entitled *The Christian's Happiness*. It forms a lovely and enduring parenthesis to Adolphe Monod's pastoral ministry.

An unexpected call

Adolphe Monod remained at the Evangelical Church of Lyons for four years as its membership and ministry continued to grow. Then an opportunity came that was clearly of the Lord. He was offered a professorship at Montauban.

In 1830, during his conflict with the consistory in Lyon, he was one of two candidates for a position at the Reformed Church's Faculty of Theology in Montauban, but the position was never filled. Then in August 1836, it was offered to him without his soliciting it. His decision to accept, when he had recently turned down another offer from the evangelical seminary in Geneva, again shows his desire to see the Awakening impact the Reformed Church of France. His congregation, seeing God's hand in the appointment, reluctantly released him.

In later years, the Evangelical Church of Lyon continued to exist side-by-side with the French Reformed congregation that had dismissed Adolphe Monod; both still exist today. Oddly, the Reformed Church of Lyon was the only congregation in the national church that was not open to Monod. The consistory would only let him preach there if he agreed *not* to hold services at the Evangelical Church — a condition he could not accept. Yet some years after his death, his widow Hannah was passing through Lyon and stopped to visit the Temple du Change, which she had not entered since her husband had been fired some thirty years before. The rack on the wall still indicated the hymns from the previous Sunday's worship service, and one of them was *The Christian's Happiness*!

7

A voice for evangelicals

(1836–1847)

A professor! How often Adolphe Monod had considered this possibility, wondering whether he was called and gifted for teaching. In Naples he rejected the idea; his faith was too weak and uncertain. After his conversion, pastoral obligations claimed his attention. Now he was able to explore this new avenue of ministry. Yet it wasn't really new. His goal in Montauban, as in his early years in Lyon, was to see deep spiritual renewal come to the Reformed Church of France. Only his method had changed. His focus had shifted from reaching individual congregations to training the next generation of pastors, who would, in turn, reach the congregations. He was, in effect, multiplying his old ministry.

Freed from the many demands of a pastoral calling, Adolphe Monod also had more time for his growing family, for developing his writing skills, and for exerting a broader

Old Bridge in Montauban

influence in the evangelical community. This was a happy and fruitful season.

A young seminary

The city of Montauban in southern France is located at the confluence of the Tescou and Tarn rivers, about halfway between the Atlantic Ocean and the Mediterranean Sea. When Monod arrived, it had a population of about 25,000, more than 18,000 of whom were Roman Catholic. A British friend recalls, 'Religious life was by no means vigorous or active. … The advent, therefore, of such a man as Adolphe Monod, a man of burning eloquence and lofty piety, to a town where religion was low and to a college where the influence of a good professor would be great, was hailed with unbounded thankfulness by those who were praying for the prosperity of Zion.'

The theological faculty at Montauban was still less than thirty years old — a young upstart compared to its Genevan counterpart, where Adolphe, his father, and his brothers had trained. While some of its initial difficulties had been overcome, it was plagued with the same tensions between evangelicals and liberals that afflicted the rest of the French Reformed Church. Adolphe Monod's appointment gave added lustre to the faculty and accorded the evangelicals a clear majority. There were six professors, of whom four were evangelical, one a liberal, and one with liberal leanings. In this regard, the situation looked hopeful for having a long-term impact on the health of the denomination. The roughly eighty students were divided more equally in their theological perspectives.

Monod's appointment was made by the government's Minister of Worship, Baron Pelet de la Lozère. If his name looks familiar, it is because his wife was one of the organizers of the Paris Bible Society which had frequently asked for Monod's advice during his time in Lyon. Before making the appointment, Baron Pelet inquired through Frédéric whether Adolphe would accept it and whether he would agree to carry out his duties in a peaceable, non-confrontational way. The official letter of nomination was accompanied by a cordial personal note from the baron.

> Some minds, prejudiced against you, will be astonished [at your appointment]. I expect the results to fully justify me and that, along with godliness, your presence on the faculty will produce fruit of peace and reconciliation at which everyone will have to rejoice.

Monod's reply was equally cordial and gracious.

> *I was all the more touched by the distinction you have just granted me in that I see there not only the minister's confidence in my all too feeble knowledge, but also, what is far more precious to me, the confidence of the man in my character, in spite of the prejudices of which I have long been the object.*

The installation of the new professor occurred on 17 November 1836, and a month later Baron Pelet again wrote to Adolphe Monod, this time expressing his pleasure in Monod's conduct and in the reception he had received. He continued:

> *I hope that, in the post where you are placed, you will contribute powerfully to procuring for us young pastors who are both godly and enlightened. No one is better able than you to give them both example and precept.*

Monod's pastoral experience was a major qualification for training pastors.

The professor

Adolphe Monod was initially named to fill the professorship in Gospel Ethics and Sacred Eloquence — the one for which he had applied six years earlier. Sacred Eloquence involves the preparation and delivery of sermons, showing that Monod was already a respected preacher. This subject suited his gifts and interests admirably, and he would have been happy to continue in it. Yet a professor hired to fill one faculty chair might later be transferred to a different one.

This happened in 1839, when the conservative professor of Hebrew died and the man they wanted to add to the faculty was uninterested in teaching the subject. To facilitate his appointment, Monod agreed to take over Hebrew, and there was a realignment of titles. The new professor was given a chair in ethics and apologetics, while Monod was to teach Hebrew and rhetoric. At least initially, he found teaching Hebrew to be quite dry and felt his own need for additional study, but perhaps his continued involvement with rhetoric was a refreshing counter-balance. In 1844, a new faculty position in New Testament Exegesis and Sacred Criticism was created, and in 1845 Adolphe Monod was assigned to fill it. This gave him greater opportunity to influence the theology of his students and, through them, of the congregations they would serve. An emphasis on the Bible had been sadly lacking in his own seminary training.

As Adolphe Monod began his teaching career, he noted in his journal what he called his *Rules for the Professorship.* He wanted his teaching to be as *biblical* as possible and as *historical* as possible, drawing lessons and examples from church history. His goal was utility more than mere logic or pedagogy. And, as in his preaching, he wanted to give a prominent place to the life of Jesus Christ. A pastor and theologian of the era wrote:

> *His influence on youth was extraordinary. He was truly a teacher in the highest sense of the word. … He did not leave a deep furrow in theological education; in truth, he merely coasted through the ethics chair, which was so suited to his aptitudes. He lacked the necessary leisure to mark his place in the study of Hebrew. … He scarcely had the time to sketch*

out his course on New Testament exegesis. Nevertheless, his teaching itself, by the austere beauty of its form, the clarity of its exposition, and the breath of life that animated it, exerted a deep influence on his disciples. It was the man and the orator who were remarkable. That was the real power of Adolphe Monod over youth. He elevated the moral ideal for them to such a height that he commanded their respect and gave them the grandest conception of the Christian and pastoral calling.

He not only won the respect of his students, he also won their friendship, a factor that greatly contributed to his spiritual influence. When the Monod family arrived in Montauban, relationships between seminary faculty and students were often strained. With Adolphe's pastoral heart, the young family decided to reach out to the students by taking the unusual step of inviting them for tea. The astonished and bewildered students met to discuss their response. Their solution? Accept the invitation but leave the professor's home as soon as tea was served! Now it was their host and hostess's turn to be confused. Eventually, however, persistence paid off, and the students became increasingly grateful for their visits. While these gatherings were pleasant, Adolphe also wanted to make them useful, so he would sometimes read aloud from classic works of French literature. His hospitality produced close and enduring relationships between teacher and students. A visitor to the seminary during those years was deeply impressed.

I recall this professor's home at Montauban where so many young students who today are pastors received such indelible impressions. Our sister [Hannah] played a considerable part in this activity of the family that was a centre of Christian life in Montauban.

Another contemporary recalls:

Though grave in his manners, he was very accessible, and made every student who was really anxious to do his best feel that in him he had a friend. … By a hint thrown out casually, or by advice given in a friendly, non-dictatorial spirit, or by a stimulating, well-timed thought, he was ready to help any young man in his studies or in the formation of his character.

The head of household

The Monod household which welcomed the students was, like that of Adolphe's parents, quite large. Three daughters and a son were born to Adolphe and Hannah in Lyon and another three daughters in Montauban. The parents also looked after a few young men entrusted to them for their education, and they took in a limited number of boarders and guests. All this helped their finances while giving them fresh opportunities for nurturing young people in their faith.

An important addition was Adolphe's sister, Adèle Babut, and her family. Adèle's husband, Édouard, had begun to suffer from a painful and debilitating illness and was forced to stop working. The Babuts, who had four children, moved to Montauban because of the mild climate of southern France, and the merging of the two families brought blessing for all. They lived on the outskirts of Montauban in a large house that had been divided into two apartments, one for each family, with a courtyard in front and a spacious garden on one side.

Édouard's condition continued to deteriorate, causing unremitting and increasing suffering before taking his life in 1848, yet one of Adolphe's daughters recalled years later that 'he never ceased to glorify God through his Christian patience. ... He loved to see [the children] around him and was glad to let himself be distracted by their games whenever God granted him some respite from his sufferings'. Adolphe was to recall and be strengthened by his brother-in-law's peaceful endurance when he too underwent intense suffering towards the end of his life. Édouard's example may well have been on Adolphe's mind when, one year after his brother-in-law's death, he said in his sermon *Who is Thirsty?*,

> *Here is a poor servant of Jesus Christ, confined for years to a bed of inactivity and pain, who sees days of suffering end only to be replaced by nights of insomnia. Very well, that is God's chosen means for more fully satisfying his thirst. With a healthy body and an easy life he would have been spared many troubles, but he would also have lost precious opportunities to prepare himself — I should have said, to be prepared — through trials, through patience, through prayer, perhaps even through contrast, to more keenly sense a deeper bliss.*

Here he was referring to the bliss that awaits us in eternity. He also noted, almost prophetically with regard to his own life, how God can use such suffering to help other Christians and to draw non-believers to himself.

Perhaps you are among those whom God seems to have chosen to be an example of a thirst that nothing is able to extinguish. Perhaps … 'your pain is unceasing and your wound incurable, refusing to be healed' (see Jeremiah 15:18). When in such circumstances your thirst is quenched — as it can be, as it must be, as it will be if you are faithful — this will clearly demonstrate that with Jesus Christ we need never despair.

Though the professor was generally reserved and even austere, he could relax within the bosom of his family. When tea was served in the evening, Adolphe would tell stories, often Bible stories, to the children. Then he would pray for the family. His prayers were 'brief, spiritual, fervent, often specifying with great minuteness and striking simplicity any particular need of the family, or mentioning by name any friend, present or absent, who was in circumstances that called forth his sympathies'. An Englishman who boarded with the family recalls:

His disposition was very affectionate, and, either by nature or as the result of careful self-discipline, his temper was most equable. … In his deportment towards his wife, he was at once most respectful and affectionate, showing great deference to her judgement and great consideration for her happiness. His love towards his children was most tender. He found pleasure in their simple tales, and was ready to enter into all their play. I think I see now his look of thorough enjoyment as his little boy came into the room one evening to take part in a game, dressed as a professor of theology. … [He declared] that in the gravest lecture he delivered, he was sure he did not look half so grave as this mimic doctor.

In later years, his children testified to the atmosphere in which they grew up.

> *Never were children loved more tenderly than his were. Never, perhaps, were children loved in a more holy way, by which we mean loved for themselves and for their true good. He was rather severe, but we don't think that any of them recalls having been punished unjustly or brusquely or in a moment of impulse. …*
>
> *Moreover, he loved to see his children cheerful and playful. … Each day he set aside time for recreation with them, when he would join in their games, either in the vast garden adjacent to the house, under the shade of a magnificent path lined with chestnut trees, or on walks in the countryside, filled with freedom and charm.*

Their family life, though harmonious, was not without pain and sorrow. In addition to Adolphe's frequent health problems and the constant suffering of his brother-in-law, Adolphe and Hannah lost one of their daughters, Constance, in 1841 just after her first birthday. Adolphe was visiting family members in Paris when he got word that Constance was gravely ill. By the time he arrived home, she had died. Adolphe wrote to his mother,

> *At the door to the house, I was met by my children running out to meet me all dressed in black. We went into the room where our child passed from this world to her Father. Kneeling in front of the bed where she suffered and where she was delivered, together with our children we called upon and blessed the God of our affliction and of our comfort.*

Faith struggled to cling to God in the midst of the pain.

> *Ask God for us not only that he subdue our hearts but that*
> *he fill us in our sorrow with a holy joy. ... I am not there yet,*
> *my poor mother. ... As soon as weather permitted, my wife*
> *and I, with our five children, visited the cemetery. ... Oh,*
> *bitterness of death! Oh, fruit of sin! Never in my life have I*
> *experienced anything like that. Oh my child! Oh my God! Oh*
> *my mother! I embraced my wife and exhorted my children,*
> *the children whom God has left me, and we prayed on our*
> *knees.*

The pain was agonizing and the battle was real, but in the end faith had the victory.

> *Oh, may God give me souls as my wages! May he remember*
> *that the field I have cultivated for his glory has been watered*
> *with our tears and with the blood of our child! ... How*
> *good the Lord is! It seems to me that I love him a bit more*
> *than before he gave us this cup to drink. May the Spirit of*
> *peace and love be poured out on our little colony at Rue de*
> *l'Hôpital!*

Monod's single-minded devotion to the things of God is reflected in another reminiscence from his personal life:

> *Though Mr Monod was, for the most part, cheerful, yet the*
> *tone of his mind certainly inclined to seriousness rather than*
> *hilarity. ... One day I dined with him and two or three other*
> *friends at his brother-in-law's. ... We were all in high spirits,*
> *and ... the conversation was of a light and humorous cast.*
> *In the afternoon he asked me to take a stroll and said, 'I*

have been thinking of the way in which we spent the dinner hour today. Although I cannot say it was wrong, I am not satisfied with it. I gladly admit that no improper sentiment was uttered — that there was nothing I could find fault with in any single anecdote or joke — but yet it seems to me that there was a grave omission. I cannot think it right that servants of Christ should meet for intercourse … and part without a single word that could edify themselves or honour their great Master.'

The preacher

Though occupied with teaching and family life, Adolphe Monod could not escape preaching. In Montauban, he was sometimes called on to occupy local pulpits, and he often gave the weekly sermon in the seminary chapel. The three-month summer break saw him making extended preaching and evangelistic tours, with shorter excursions during the two-week Easter recess. He was again Monod the evangelist, Monod the spokesman for the Awakening. Touring, in part, to raise funds for the evangelical societies, he travelled through France and sometimes into Switzerland, England, and the Channel Islands.

The schedule was strenuous. He might preach two or three times in a day. One Sunday service in Montpellier lasted for four hours, including one and a half hours for serving communion. The next year, he wrote from Marseilles:

Sunday morning I preached in the Great Temple at Nîmes to a very attentive audience of two thousand persons. The

Lord sustained me well. (The Authority of God's Word, Luke 4:1-11). After the service, it had been arranged that I should preach for Mr Gallup at three o'clock. Thus I preached a second time in the Small Temple. In the evening, there was a meeting at the home of Mrs Dhauteville (1 John 5). I was given a good, fine day, which I ended by visiting the poor blessed Blanc, from Saint-Gilles, who is dying of facial cancer.

One evening he arrived around eight or nine o'clock to spend the night at the home of a pastor friend who had offered him lodging as he passed through. The friend asked, 'What time would you like to preach tomorrow?' but the traveller replied that he had to leave early the next morning, as he was expected elsewhere. His host was undaunted. Ignoring Monod's protests, he had the church bell rung, calling the congregation out of bed to hear the famous preacher. And they came.

For Adolphe Monod, preaching was not an intellectual or cerebral affair. He poured himself into his messages. 'I would like to have a rigid rule that I only preach in the temples one day out of two. It is neither the body nor the mind that is exhausted; it is the soul. The emotions involved in preaching such as mine are too strong to be renewed every day.'

His published sermons from this period are as varied as his audiences. When preaching in the various churches around Montauban and especially on his preaching tours, his messages were often designed to bring nominal Christians into a living, personal faith in Christ. In *The Philippian Jailer,* he drew his listeners' attention to the jailer's conversion and said:

I offer [this conversion] for your attention today not so that you will ponder with sterile emotion the grace God showed to this poor pagan, but in order to bring you — you who call yourselves Christians — to the point of laying hold of this same salvation. ... Neither your birth nor your baptism makes you a child of God, a true disciple of Jesus Christ. 'You must be born again.' ... Here I am, ready to bring you the pure doctrine of Jesus Christ, as the apostles did to the jailer, provided that you bring to me, as the jailer did to the apostles, a heart that sighs after salvation.

He also strove to awaken the desire for such a conversion. In his paradoxical *The Happiness of the Christian Life*, he showed the blessings that abound in that life, even in what appear, at first glance, to be some of its harder, more austere aspects. Later, in his famous sermon *God is Love*, he made the all-too-familiar story of God's breath-taking sacrifice for us come freshly alive.

That death, that torture, that broken body, that shed blood, those insults are, without doubt, bitter aspects of the cross. But the real bitterness lies elsewhere. The cause of the sweat of blood lies elsewhere; the cup that he asked, if possible, to be spared from drinking lies elsewhere. The real bitterness of the cross is sin coming upon him along with what follows from sin: the Father's wrath and the Father's curse.

Other sermons dealt with more sensitive topics. In *Money's Friend*, Monod carefully described all the varied forms that greed can take, exposing them as a kind of idolatry that is serious in its consequences and widespread among Christians. In *The Demoniacs* he confronted a topic that is clear in Scripture but also ridiculed in modern society and avoided by many Christians. Disposing of possible sources for such avoidance, he went on to warn us that, in order not to fall into the devil's traps, we must battle, be on our guard, and pray.

The theme of battling against Satan appears again in what are perhaps Monod's most important sermons from this period: his series *Jesus Tempted in the Wilderness*. Given in the seminary chapel, they contain cogent warnings and sound advice, some of which were aimed specifically at the students, but most of which apply to all believers. Monod first alerts us to the inevitability of temptation, then assures us that Christ's victory in the wilderness guarantees that we can be victorious, and finally shows us how to discern and combat the underlying nature of the enemy's strategies — the temptations to distrust, unfaithfulness, and presumption — using God's Word as our only weapon.

One other important teaching from this period is worth mentioning. Beginning in Lyon, as we saw, Adolphe Monod began inviting believers to less formal times of Bible teaching. There he felt he could go into greater depth than in a general worship service. In Montauban, these teachings occurred in the Sunday afternoon services in the seminary chapel. One series of meditations was what he called *Explanation of Saint Paul's Epistle to the Ephesians*. The content is part commentary, part devotional, part exhortation. His goal was 'to seek … the sacred author's thought, which is, for us, the thought of God himself; then, having found that thought, to receive it with childlike simplicity and expound it to our listeners with the trembling faithfulness of an interpreter of the Holy Spirit'. Published posthumously from his notes, this unique work displays both Monod's impressive scholarship and his warm pastoral heart.

The author

Even with his teaching and preaching responsibilities, Adolphe Monod found time for writing during the Montauban years. As a prominent evangelical pastor, he continued to contribute to the *Correspondance fraternelle* (also called the *Correspondance pastorale fraternelle* or *Correspondance évangélique*). Begun in 1833 and coordinated by Pastor Alphonse de Frontin, this informal publication was intended for like-minded pastors who were continuing the work of the Awakening. Monod's participation began later that first year, while he was still in Lyon, but he had more time for it in Montauban. Eventually about one hundred pastors contributed, sharing what they were doing and discussing issues related to church practice and growth. In 1839, Monod's notes on public and private worship, first prepared for his seminary students, were distributed as chapters in the *Correspondance*. He argued that preaching should put far less emphasis on oratory than on engaging and helping the congregants.

A more significant work from this period is his popular book *Lucile, or Reading the Bible*. It was written in 1841 as part of a competition organized by the Religious Book Society of Toulouse. The first part of each entry was to be a brief argument for the authority of the Bible as God's Word. Then the books were to advocate everyone's freedom to read the Scriptures for themselves.

God was preparing Adolphe Monod to write *Lucile* long before the competition was established. In evangelizing Roman Catholics in Lyon, he was drawn, almost against his will, into a series of public dialogues on doctrine that eventually turned into debates. As part of his preparation, he studied Catholic theology in order to discern what was in accord with Scripture and what was false and erroneous. He also had the occasion to meet godly Catholics, some of whom were priests. His dedication to these dialogues is all the more remarkable when one remembers France's long and bloody history of animosity between Catholics and Protestants.

Lucile takes the form of discussions and correspondence between Lucile de Lassalle, her husband, the Roman Catholic Abbé Flavian, and Mr Mercier, an evangelical Christian recently converted from Catholicism. Though written as fiction, the book is based on the conversion of 'Mr and Mrs M.' and of Mr Merlin of Thionville. There are published letters from Monod to the Ms, encouraging them in their new walk of faith and offering spiritual counsel.

The book opens with Lucile writing to the abbot to explain her longing for spiritual convictions. She has just recognized her own religious indifference and reports that her husband is completely unbelieving. The godly cleric's reply expresses his desire to meet with her and her husband to address her concerns. The book is then divided into two parts. Part 1, 'The Inspiration of Scripture', consists of two extended dialogues in which Abbé Flavian convinces Lucile of the Bible's authenticity and authority as the foundation for Roman Catholicism. Her husband continues to espouse the natural religion of Rousseau, though he is shaken by the arguments he has heard.

Part 2, 'The Interpretation of Scripture', is given in the form of letters. Lucile is fully persuaded that Jesus is God's Son and that Holy Scripture is divinely inspired, and she longs to read the Bible for herself. Her local curate has forbidden her to obtain a Bible from the Protestant colporteurs, because their Bibles are 'altered', so she pleads with Mr Flavian to send her a true Bible. The abbot confesses that the Bibles sold by the colporteurs, though lacking the Apocryphal books, are otherwise authentic. However, he argues that at her stage of spiritual development she must rely on the Roman Catholic church to interpret it for her and to direct what parts of it she reads and when. At this point a family friend, Mr Mercier, visits the de Lassalles. He has been in just the state that Lucile is in and has found great light for his soul in reading the Scriptures. Both Lucile and her husband are amazed to find that their guest has become a totally new person since his conversion. The rest of the book consists of letters between Lucile and Mr Mercier. The latter responds at great length to all the Catholic 'proofs' of the existence and need for a church body as the infallible interpreter of Scripture, and he refutes the abbot's arguments on the dangers of reading the Bible for oneself. In her last letter, Lucile tells him that she has read the New Testament and found real peace in her heart, along with an assurance of her salvation.

Lucile is a masterful work of apologetics that shared the prize in the competition with *Man Faced with* [or *Confronted by*] *the Bible* by Philippe Boucher. To Adolphe Monod's surprise, *Lucile* was received with great enthusiasm and enjoyed continued popularity for decades, eventually being translated into English and a number of other languages.

Beyond France and Switzerland

During this period, Adolphe Monod's reputation was extending well beyond the confines of France and French-speaking Switzerland.

In 1842, illness led him to seek treatment at the health spa at Gräfenberg in Austrian Silesia. He travelled with Hannah and their son William. The Monods were charmed by this remote and backward area, where the customs officials were frightened of books and carefully inspected all the ones they brought. They left Montauban sometime in July, and the trip lasted through part of October. Their outbound voyage, facilitated by the marvellous innovation of railways, included visits to many important sites in Reformation history. After the six-week 'cure', they returned to Montauban, with stops in Halle, Berlin, and Wittenberg so that Adolphe could meet with leading German evangelicals. While he apparently did not engage in ministry on this trip (a rare occurrence), these few months made a lasting impression and are recounted in great detail in the memoirs the family published. Monod particularly noted the disciplined and efficient way his German colleagues pursued their studies and writing.

The year 1842 also saw the College of New Jersey (now Princeton University) award him a Doctor in Divinity degree 'in consideration of your attainments in Sacred Literature and Theological Science and also of your distinguished labours in the cause of truth and righteousness'. His reputation had crossed the Atlantic, though he never did.

His growing international stature is confirmed by his involvement with the Evangelical Alliance. He was invited to attend its organizational meeting in London in the summer of 1846. While extremely sympathetic to their goal of displaying Christian unity, he expressed concern that trying to take united action (for instance, publishing a journal) might compromise that unity. A week of preliminary meetings beginning on 12 August set the stage for the two weeks of the main conference. Adolphe Monod participated actively all three weeks.

The conference drew nearly a thousand participants from the British Isles and North America, with a smaller number from the Continent. Some fifty denominations were represented. Monod was one of ten representatives from France (four from the established church), and on the first day of the main meeting, he addressed the assembly on behalf of his countrymen. The delegates discussed many contentious issues, while still trying to exhibit the brotherly love they had gathered to proclaim. Sensitive topics included how broadly to define the Alliance's theology and whether they should adopt a confession of faith. Throughout the meetings, Adolphe Monod provided a strong voice for moderation and compromise, cautioning delegates to move forward with humility but also with confidence in their ultimate success. He wrote, 'The principle of the Alliance is none other than ... to lift up brotherly love and return it, in the eyes of the Church and the world, to the place that it has lost in the Christianity of our age. ... I could not bear the thought that such a work would be carried out in our day and I remain a stranger to it.'

Following the meeting, a large number of the delegates from a variety of denominations attended a communion service in London.

> *This was a touching and solemn scene that I will never forget. 'This is heavenly', the venerable Dr Bunting, president of the Methodists, said to me. Leaving from there we went to visit a school for poor girls whom Mrs Kinnaird is training to be servants. About sixty young girls, aged eighteen to twenty down to six or seven, were arranged in front of me according to height, with the smallest in the first row. Arrayed in simple, clean attire, they were singing a hymn. When I saw them, I was deeply moved. Right in front of me was a charming little girl, about six years old, no more, who opened her little mouth to sing like the others. The refrain was,* And crown Him Lord of all. *When I heard those dear children inviting angels, men, Jews, Gentiles, and the Christian church to crown the Lord, my weak heart broke, and I could only cry instead of singing. That's when I truly sensed that Jesus Christ is the true God, the living God, since he is the God of the little children. ... Ah, it is with the heart that one believes, not with the understanding, and all the sacred criticism is not worth the little six-year-old who was facing me opening her mouth to tell the angels, Jews, Gentiles, and Christians,* And crown Him Lord of all!

Monod stayed on in Great Britain for several more weeks, meeting with other evangelicals, visiting friends and family, and preaching in English in Edinburgh, Liverpool, and Manchester to raise funds for The Religious Book Society of Toulouse.

A return to pastoral ministry

Adolphe Monod's seminary life was interrupted by another call from God in the spring of 1847. He had been considering a return to pastoral ministry, where his main talent and calling lay, and he was concerned for the education of his children, especially his son, William. Beyond that, due to changes at the seminary, he felt that his influence as a professor had been reduced considerably. Someone in the family, perhaps Frédéric, had mentioned the possibility of Adolphe joining Frédéric on the staff of the Reformed Church of Paris, but Adolphe thought it unlikely that the consistory would vote to hire him. He was wrong. He was unexpectedly offered the post of suffragan pastor, aiding Henri François Juillerat, the 65-year-old president of the consistory. The offer was especially attractive in that pastor Juillerat was anxious to have Monod take over his preaching responsibilities.

Attractive though the offer was, Monod took time to pray and earnestly seek God's will. In the end, however, the decision was clear. God had opened a door, and it was his job to walk through it. The Montauban years had been happy and fruitful, but it was time to move on. The offer from Paris was received in April 1847, and Adolphe moved his family in late September.

8

Preaching and pain

(1847–1855)

It was a homecoming of sorts. Adolphe Monod's father had passed away in 1836, while Adolphe was still in Lyon, but his mother and most of his siblings were living in Paris, and Frédéric was already a titular pastor in the Reformed Church there. They would work together. The move was a special joy for Louise, who had only a few more years to live. This devoted mother of 'the twelve sparrows' had an especially close bond with Adolphe, perhaps because of their prayers for one another during their respective spiritual crises.

Adolphe was welcomed almost as warmly by the consistory as by his family. Contrary to his expectations, the vote to hire him had been nearly unanimous. With eight pastors and eight elders voting by secret ballot, there was just one abstention, 'as if one didn't dare write those three letters, *non*'. One of the elders was Count Pelet de la Lozère (formerly a baron), who had appointed Adolphe to his post in Montauban. Another elder was so overjoyed at Monod's selection, he insisted on writing the formal letter to the candidate and mailing it himself that same evening. Frédéric wrote a happy letter to his brother, expressing how he sensed God's hand confirming the move. Finally Mr Juillerat, for whom Adolphe would be working and who had asked that he be appointed, wrote to his future suffragan:

> You have won confidence through your moderation and wisdom. There is a vast field of work here and many hearts that want you, many good wishes calling out to you. It is costing me more than I can say to step down from the pulpit, but nothing could console me to it more than to see you step up in my place.

This was a far happier situation than he had encountered with the consistory in Lyon, and there was a general expectation that he would be asked to fill the next titular vacancy on the pastoral staff. This expectation was fulfilled two years later in an unexpected way.

Pastoral ministry

If Adolphe Monod wanted more opportunity to preach, he certainly got it; the schedule was gruelling. The entire city was organized as one large parish, with tens of thousands of members spread among three houses of worship and served by a team of pastors who shared many of the duties on a rotating basis.

Temple de l'Oratoire du Louvre

Monod's Sunday preaching carried him to distant corners of the metropolis. At seven a.m., he was called to speak at a secondary school, the Lycée Louis-le-Grand, where he was the chaplain. He was also the first chaplain for the prison of Saint-Lazare where he often preached. Then he would return home to prepare himself to preach at the noon worship service at one of the main worship centres. The largest of these buildings was the Temple de l'Oratoire du Louvre; the second was the Temple de Pentemont, located on the Left Bank; the third and smallest was the Temple de Sainte Marie, near the Place de la Bastille. That was where Adolphe and Billy had preached while seminary students. Part of Sunday afternoon was taken up with visiting the poor and the sick. Then, on Sunday evening, Adolphe was involved with a much smaller and less formal gathering at the Church of the Oratoire. The evening meeting was started by Frédéric and later taught by Adolphe. Those who came tended to be spiritually hungry, and it was there that detailed Bible teaching could occur. Many of Adolphe's catechism students became part of this group, which, in a sense, formed his real 'parish', the place where he felt most at home.

Adolphe Monod expressed his sense of calling for this period in a letter to his old friend and encourager, Countess Pelet.

> *Your point of view with regard to my ministry is in such perfect agreement with mine! Reserve my limited strength to make the most of my personal gift; then join to preaching those pastoral duties that have an essentially spiritual nature. In other words,* devote myself to the Word and to prayer, *that is the desire of my heart. … Now we need to ask the Lord to make me faithful, in the true sense of the word, which is far from being exhausted by simply having my doctrine agree with the orthodox system. … As to your desire that I might place myself as a conciliator between the various factions of evangelical Christianity, that is one of my constant prayers. … One more desire of my ministry is to work in my private interactions for the growth of … men of an elevated spirit who are open to the things of God.*

Crisis in the nation; crisis in the church

These ministry desires were ultimately fulfilled, but not before political events altered life in Paris. Less than six months after Adolphe and his family arrived in Paris, the revolution of February 1848 ushered in France's Second Republic and a new period of political instability. After several days of protests and then violence, the new government began to emerge, and elections for the national assembly were scheduled for Easter Sunday. French Protestants had differing reactions to the revolution. Adolphe Monod was cautious, hoping that it might bring about a separation of church and state along with needed social reforms, but he saw many problems and pitfalls ahead. Some Protestants wanted to see a pastor in the new national assembly and urged Monod to put his name forward, but he in no way felt either called to or suited for such service. He remained a faithful citizen but jealously avoided anything that would compromise his spiritual and pastoral influence. He was a pastor, not a politician.

Then came the June uprising. Adolphe was on a preaching tour in southern France when he got news of the fighting in Paris. An intense and bloody battle took place in the neighbourhood of Faubourg Poissonnière where the family lived. Adolphe's mother, Louise, wrote to Billy, 'Hannah saw her apartment invaded by the national guard, who fired from the windows on the insurgents. The panes were broken but none of them suffered the least harm. Our Hannah gave proof once again of calm and courage, but how much she must have suffered from Adolphe's absence at such a moment! He is more to be pitied for finding himself so far from home, where he will no doubt return without delay.' He did return, cutting short his trip, and was relieved to find his family safe. Frédéric's neighbourhood had remained quiet, but Adolphe's younger brother Gustave, a surgeon, was constantly called to help the wounded. At one point, he was crossing the Place de La Fayette when bullets whistled past his head, fortunately missing him.

Given the state's control over religion, the Reformed Church of France also experienced crisis. A general assembly was convened for the following September to consider a desired reorganization. Adolphe and Frédéric were both delegates to the assembly, as was their younger brother Horace, who was a pastor in the national church in Marseille. (Billy, the fourth pastor among the Monod brothers, was serving in a church in Lausanne, Switzerland.) The main doctrinal issue to be addressed in the assembly was the adoption of a new confession of faith. The liberal majority wanted doctrinal heterodoxy — unity based solely on tradition — and thus did not want to write or adopt a confession. Most of those touched by the Awakening felt that it was important to have a strong confession of faith and were in favour of revising or replacing the historic *Confession of La Rochelle*. The latter group was further divided as to the necessity of doing so immediately. When the assembly voted not to adopt a confession of faith, Frédéric and Count Agénor de Gasparin resigned from the meeting and walked out. Adolphe took a more moderate position. He felt that because no action had been taken, the *Confession of La Rochelle* had not been abrogated and was still the doctrinal standard of the national church.

Early in the new year, the Paris consistory received a letter from Frédéric, resigning from the Reformed Church of France. He and Count de Gasparin formally withdrew and founded the Union of Free Evangelical Churches. Frédéric was asked to reconsider his resignation, but nothing new could be found to induce him to change his mind. What was Adolphe to do? His theology, like Frédéric's, was obviously that of the Awakening, but were there sufficient grounds for schism? His desire to see unity displayed within the body of Christ had impelled his involvement in forming the Evangelical Alliance, and it weighed heavily on him here. After much earnest prayer, he remained in the national church to work for change within it, as did most other evangelicals.

This institutional separation, though merely external, was deeply painful to both brothers. There were no hard feelings. They simply concluded that the Lord was calling them to different work, and when the Constituent Assembly of the new denomination was held in Paris in the autumn, Adolphe invited all of its members to a gathering in his home. Later in 1849, Adolphe was appointed to fill Frédéric's former position as a titular pastor in the Reformed Church of Paris, and his efforts towards renewal continued. Yet Adolphe did not accept this new position without deep emotion.

> How can it be that I should today take the place of this older brother, this faithful disciple, this pastor respected by all in his resignation and honoured by all in his sacrifice? I could well tell myself that my presence in the post that he occupied for so long is one more token, through the circumstance that led to it, of the brotherly affection that unites us one to the other as tenderly as ever. My soul is crushed by the thought of even an apparent separation.

Why did Adolphe Monod stay in the national church in Paris when he had founded an independent evangelical church in Lyon? Many asked that question, and some accused him of wanting to take over Frédéric's position. In fact, Adolphe's actions were completely consistent with his decision in Lyon. In both cases he prayed earnestly for God's wisdom. In Lyon, he left the national church only after he was fired from his post, and only then did he consider founding an independent congregation. In 1849, he was not forced to resign. In published remarks, he argued that he could not leave a post to which God had clearly assigned him, except 'for reasons that are so clear and so decisive that I have no right to remain'. In his view, neither the actions of the September assembly nor the very nature of the situation met this criterion. Though he, like Frédéric, regarded the then-current state of the church as untenable in the long term, he felt the need for patience. He saw definite signs of progress and reasons for hope, noting the increased number of faithful pastors and the growth of various Bible and mission societies. 'When I come before Jesus Christ and consult him in the spirit on the question, "Should I give my resignation?" I always come to the same result, "No, I definitely should not." ... Thus I remain today, ready to leave tomorrow if tomorrow shows me the impossibility of remaining in full faithfulness.'

Family trials

While the nation and the church were going through difficult times, the Monod family had its own trials. Their joy at being reunited in Paris was punctuated by more sombre events.

The first was the death of Adolphe's brother-in-law, Édouard Babut. Adolphe visited the Babuts in Montauban at the start of his trip through southern France in the summer of 1848. The affection that had developed between the brothers-in-law was deep, and Adolphe was distressed to observe in a letter, 'What a life you have! Out of seven days, not even half an hour of calm, of real relief!' Adolphe hoped to end his trip with another stop in Montauban before returning to Paris, but the June uprising necessitated his return to his endangered family. In July it became clear that Édouard's time on earth was coming to an end. Adolphe wrote to his beloved friend.

> *My dear Édouard, do I need to tell you with what painful sympathy we are following you in these new crises of physical suffering and mental anguish? Or with what edification and consolation we have learned* the Lord's goal *and of the humble submission he has given you to his mysterious will? Oh, my dear friend, if the gospel is true — and we know it is true — this submission is* the one thing necessary *for you, whatever the nature of your trial is or could be or might become. 'I am giving you counsel that I can scarcely receive myself,' I who bear my ten-pound weight less patiently than you bear your hundred-pound weight. Yet the counsel is true because it is the gospel! It is not possible for it to be impossible to accept the will of God peacefully! … What will my poor preaching be beside that of a member of Jesus Christ, beaten down day and night as you are and yet never ceasing to give glory to God!*

In the face of such peaceful endurance, we stand on holy ground that few of us have had to tread. Little did Adolphe realize that his brother-in-law's patience and faith were to be a model for his own in less than a decade. Édouard Babut finally reached the end of his suffering on 3 October 1848. He was sixty-one years old. His wife, Adèle, had little to retain her in Montauban and soon moved to Paris, where she and her older daughter, Marie (just turning twenty-one), lived with Frédéric, while their younger daughter, Fanny, lived with Adolphe and Hannah.

The next loss occurred in 1851 with the death of Adolphe's mother, Louise. Her spiritual malaise had resolved before this, and, by her own declaration, she died in great peace. Her last illness was brief, beginning in late February and ending on 4 March. Ten of her children and many of her grandchildren were there. Frédéric was incapacitated during her final days on earth, so it was Adolphe who gave his mother pastoral care. Her faith never wavered. She asked each of her descendants to write out a passage from the Bible for her to read and dwell on. The day of her death, she observed that nobody had given her Isaiah 44:22: 'I have blotted out your transgressions like a cloud and your sins like mist.' This was her hope and her faith, and she asked that the verse be read to her. Her children wanted to have it engraved on her tomb, but, perhaps for reasons of space, a shorter quote from Isaiah 43:1 was used. It reads, 'I have redeemed you; you are mine.'

The following year, it seemed as if Adolphe's wife, Hannah, might be taken from them. In July 1852, she and 'M', presumably their oldest daughter, Mary, were out shopping on a Wednesday afternoon when Hannah suffered what was termed a stroke. Mary, then about twenty-one years old, brought her mother home unconscious, and the situation looked grave. Adolphe's distress is reflected in a telegraphic letter to a dear friend.

Her speech lost; no movement or feeling in part of her left side. Imminent danger. My brother Gustave [the surgeon] said to Frédéric ... 'There is a possibility that she will come back from it.' To see her die and die without communicating with me, oh my friend! My soul melts in anguish!

That same evening the most serious symptoms stopped. They disappeared gradually. Gustave took heart. ... Thursday midday, a consultation. Mr Rayer considered the case to be quite serious, almost desperate. Friday, notable improvement. ... My children and I were kept in peace. We, I too, I had absolutely no bitterness. I considered that God was just if he struck and good if he spared. ...

Pray for us and keep on praying. I still don't dare give myself over to hope. Imagine poor Adolphe Monod without his life's companion, the pillar of his home, the helper of his ministry, the balance in his advice, the dear friend of his heart, and the mother of his children!

Here, as with the loss of their daughter Constance, we see faith battling with fear and then emerging victorious. In this case, God spared Hannah, who recovered and lived another sixteen years. She was able to resume a normal life, though without the full strength she had previously possessed.

His preaching

But life and work go on, even in the face of death and family crisis. A large part of Adolphe's work was preaching aimed at bringing new spiritual vitality into the church. In his explanation of why he remained in the Reformed

Church of France, Adolphe commented on the state of the Awakening.

> *The first phase of the Awakening ... is giving way to a new phase, whose end is not yet well determined. ... Charged with reviving an almost-extinct faith, it has seemed more concerned with enlightening than regenerating. ... Alas, it is only too possible for the head to believe without the heart being touched or the life renewed! ... It is not that the Awakening has failed to produce good fruit of true holiness. ... But ... external action and the Christianity of works have taken the place of pre-eminence that belongs only to the internal life and to spiritual Christianity. ... One can join the movement and take a prominent position in it without being a man of prayer, without 'hungering and thirsting after righteousness,' ... without penetrating to the very heart of the gospel.*

These are sad words that have a too familiar ring in our day. In the face of this situation, Monod's calling was to both preach and live a heart-penetrating gospel that would change lives.

Preach he did. This final phase of Adolphe Monod's public ministry produced many of his most beloved sermons, and it is here that we see him best as a preacher. As one contemporary put it, 'His appearance in the Protestant pulpit was an event. ... Up until Adolphe Monod, at least in France, the evangelical movement had had witnesses, sometimes almost apostles, such as Felix Neff, but not yet an orator in the full sense of the word.' Another recalled, 'I was then twelve to fifteen years old, an age when one can scarcely listen to a discourse, much less a sermon, without impatience to see it end. Those of Adolphe Monod always lasted more than an hour and sometimes an hour and a half, yet they never seemed long to me. They made such a deep, living impression on me that … in reading his printed sermons, I note minor changes in entire sentences that have stayed with me.'

What were the qualities that made Monod 'the voice of the Awakening'? Some of them related to his pulpit demeanour. 'Adolphe Monod did not have a majestic presence. He was of average height with irregular features, but he bore the mark of a high moral distinction, enhanced by the seriousness appropriate for deep souls. His smile was wonderful; it was a light. The spoken word transfigured him as it does all the great masters of eloquence.' His voice was said to have a pleasing 'golden' tone. Yet all these qualities were only the vehicle for conveying his message; they cannot explain the enduring interest in reading his sermons.

One key to his influence is common to all great servants of God: prayer. 'His preparation was, above all, a prayer. … In going over his manuscripts, one finds him frequently interrupting his composition with exclamations such as, "Oh Christ, help me through the blood of the cross!"' Such prayers stemmed from a deep desire to bring glory to God alone.

I sometimes fear that the ability to speak that the Lord has given me might hinder his being glorified in me. I need to pray all the more lest perhaps I will be all the less useful. Moreover, I can say to God's glory that the thought of preaching with no other fruit than the praise of man is antipathetic to me. It is not only a detestable sin in my eyes, but the most miserable of all miseries. Oh my God, grant that I might not be a clanging cymbal!

Such lengthy, prayerful sermon preparation took much time that he would gladly have spent in personal ministry with members of his flock. Perhaps this explains his exclamation, 'Oh cross of preaching the cross!'

While Monod's language was classic and timeless, it was never cold. 'It was very much alive and very much his. The depths of his soul breathed in it.' He followed his own rule of never putting more ardour into his delivery than was in his heart, but his heart had boundless ardour for God and for his Word.

Monod's sermons departed in two respects from Calvin's model. First, he embraced the use of eloquence. This might seem to contradict his 1839 statement that sermons should have less emphasis on oratory, yet Monod made a clear distinction between oratory and eloquence.

Far be it from me to refuse Saint Paul all the natural gifts of eloquence. We cannot doubt that he had … the loveliest of them — clarity of thought, forcefulness of idea, strong emotion, choice of expression, warmth and liveliness of language. … Yet Saint Paul must have lacked certain external gifts, which are of only secondary importance for the reflective person but which make up the glory and prize of speaking in the eyes of the ordinary person — the gifts of strength, voice quality, action, sparkle. Paul was a man of great eloquence

> *in the most elevated sense of the term, but Paul was not a*
> *great orator in the popular meaning of this title.*

In Monod's eyes, eloquence in a sermon had to exist, not for its own sake, but as a servant of the gospel.

The second way his sermons departed from Calvin's model is that they were not a rigorous exposition of a passage of Scripture. Though he quoted extensively from the Bible, his sermon text was often no more than a verse or a phrase. He saved detailed exposition for less formal settings.

His sermons also contain an unusual mixture of firmness and humility that is best explained by the word 'mystery'. Monod recognized that there are questions to which God has chosen not to give us clear answers in his Word, and on those questions he humbly avoided speculation or human opinion, choosing to leave them as mysteries. Yet where Scripture is clear, whether in doctrine or application, he was firm and direct.

Monod's sermon introductions were short, free of humour and of 'the hateful me'. He moved directly to the point of his discourse. This practice reflected the seriousness with which he regarded the proclamation of the gospel. Preaching was, for him, a sacred responsibility. Yet his deep, intense seriousness, his unwillingness to amuse his listeners, far from turning them off to his messages, seemed to hold their rapt attention.

If his messages were serious, they were also winsome. Scripture sets a very high standard for the Christian life, and so did Adolphe Monod, but he made that standard appear attractive, not burdensome. Perhaps this is his greatest gift. He made it clear that the Christian life is one of self-denial and renouncement, yet his vivid portrayal of its joys and privileges made that life seem totally desirable. In the national church in Lyon, his youthful zeal led him to try to push people into God's kingdom by depicting the consequences of sin; in his mature years, he tried to draw them in by painting the wonders of God's love for us as expressed on the cross. His deep love for God and his genuine love and concern for his listeners gave warmth to his sermons.

His message

His main subject matter — the gospel — was characteristic of the preaching sparked by the Awakening, but his sermons display an unusual and beautiful balance between heart and mind. Many in his audiences had heard and even believed the gospel, but they needed to know Christ. Sometimes his message was quite direct, as in his famous sermon, *Give Me Your Heart.*

> *Who have I been entreating and for what? Has it been for God to pardon sinful man and give him his heart, which is all too justly alienated from us? No, I have been entreating sinful man to give his heart to the God of Jesus Christ; to the God for whom that heart hungers and thirsts; to the God who has fully given us his own heart; to the God who seems to have need of ours in order to complete his bliss of love. ...*

Oh, my brother, my sister, give the world today the only moral spectacle more lovely than that of an angel who has never stopped loving God. Give it the spectacle of a sinner, an enemy who has become a friend. … Man refuses God's heart every day, but God has never refused man's heart. He doesn't solicit it, awaken it, and touch it in order to refuse it. Only desire, and you will give him your heart. Desire, and you have already given it.

As for you, elder brothers who have already returned, go and embrace that prodigal child retracing the path to the father's home. 'Greet [him] with the kiss of love.' Encourage his still wavering steps. Above all, above all, spare him the scandal of your dead profession and know for certain whether you yourselves have truly given your hearts to God!

Sometimes his appeal was less direct, but always he preached the cross and God's love for us. In 1853, he sensed the need to remind his listeners of the fundamentals of Christian doctrine and to separate those truths from common errors. Thus he gave a series of discourses on doctrine taken from the life of Jesus Christ. His desire was always for Christ, the living Word, to come first in his preaching, with the Bible, the written Word, right behind it. All else was subsidiary.

Yet it was also important for him to relate the gospel to the special needs of his congregants. After arriving in Paris, he at first had difficulty finding the right 'vein' for his preaching — the themes God wanted him to emphasize. The uncertainties of the times weighed on him as they did on others, and he sometimes resorted to reworking sermons he had delivered during his time in Montauban. For instance, in 1846 he had given a message called *Fatalism* that 'created a particular sensation. I seem to have touched on a sensitive point for the current generation.' This reaction apparently prompted him to revisit the subject for the Parisian Christians because a published sermon dating from April 1848 bears the same title.

Other sermons were likewise designed to meet people where they were. In 1848, a pair of sermons on *Woman, Her Mission and Her Life* addressed an issue almost as important in his day as in ours. In 1849, after the revolution of the previous year and the upheaval it produced in all segments of society, he preached two sermons on what a Christian was to do when faced with *Foundations in Ruins*. And he even published two children's sermons. He knew how to connect with the real life concerns of his listeners.

The weight of illness

If Adolphe Monod's preaching was designed to meet the concerns of others, he had needs of his own; he continued to struggle with his health. At the time of the assembly of the Reformed Church of France in September 1848, he was sufficiently ill that he considered not attending, but this was the same kind of problem that had plagued him before. It was in 1851, following the death of his mother, that things began to change. He and those close to him began to sense a growing weakness and fatigue. That first year, 1851, saw him travel to England for a regular ecumenical gathering of the Evangelical Alliance. He was also entering a time of intense ministry, frequently preaching at worship services, ordinations, dedications, and the like. And so he struggled on. A lover of nature, he often retreated to the countryside when he needed to attend to urgent work or compose a new sermon. In the summer of 1852, he made his last preaching tour, though he continued to take other trips as a way of resting and regaining strength. He could no longer meet all his ministry obligations, and he relied heavily on the help of his friend Pastor Petit, who graciously took on some of his responsibilities.

Then in 1854, as his second daughter, Louise Marguerite, was getting married, the situation began to look more ominous. When weeks of rest spent at Le Havre brought no improvement, the doctors recommended a water cure at Évian. He went in July and expected to return to Paris in late October, but the doctors advised against it, instead sending him to Divonne for an additional one month 'cure'. This too was ineffective, and Adolphe Monod returned to Paris in November. All told, he had been gone for six months.

He continued to preach as he was able, including on Christmas and the following Easter, but each sermon was becoming a major effort. A listener recalls that a physical crisis once overcame him as he was delivering his message. He stopped abruptly, came down from the pulpit, and staggered to the sacristy. There he rested for fifteen minutes before he could conclude his sermon.

He also taught his catechism classes, a task he enjoyed and felt was a crucial part of his ministry. The class ended with his Easter sermon, *I Am the Resurrection and the Life*, and

Adolphe Monod 1855

he preached only one more time after that, at Pentecost on 27 May 1855. His title was *Water Welling up to Eternal Life*, and his text was from John 4:14. His message? The water that Jesus Christ gives to the believer is *in him*, it is internal; it is *a spring* and, therefore, a permanent source of supply; and it is *welling up*, it is alive and active, jealous to be poured out. Thus his last sermons were filled with thoughts of abundant life both here and in eternity.

Prior to Pentecost, as his health continued to decline, Adolphe Monod was granted a several-month leave of absence to try to regain his strength, but even as he preached, he acknowledged that he might not be able to return.

> *Yes, my faithful friends in Christ, I am confident that this illness is for God's glory and that, whether healed or not, it will make me better able to serve God according to his will.*

He was not to be healed of his physical ailment, and his health continued to decline. In late August, the Evangelical Alliance was meeting in Paris, but he was too ill to attend.

In late September his doctors finally knew for certain the seriousness of his condition and alerted the family. The patient was not informed but managed to pry the diagnosis from one of his children. He was suffering from terminal liver cancer. He was not surprised, having sensed the growing concern of his physicians; he was, however, relieved to have the matter settled.

> *Oh my God! If you withdraw me, I know in whom I have believed. If my hour is marked out, I will bless you for it from the depths of my heart, because I know that it is much better for me to go from this world to the Father.*

His new and final ministry was about to begin — a ministry born of his suffering.

9

Farewells

(1855–1856)

How much time was left in Adolphe Monod's earthly life? No one knew. All they knew was that it would not be long and that it would be a time of intense and increasing pain. It was an emotional adjustment for everyone in the family, but especially for the patient. He prayed much, and he prayed fervently. He cried out for mercy. He cried out for healing. The battle was real, and it was intense. Yet, as when his daughter died, as when his brother-in-law's suffering neared its end, as when he feared that Hannah's stroke might prove fatal, God's grace allowed his faith to prevail.

The work of your grace is still weak in me, but whatever I do, I will always remain well below the divine example. Besides, I know that I am washed in the blood of Christ and that my body is the dwelling place of the Holy Spirit. Thus it is a question of more or less. But, oh my God, is my work finished? You alone know. It seems to me that it is not. I would have liked to leave some enduring monument for your glory! I have so many unfinished writings I would like to have finished, so many incomplete works I would like to have completed! Yet if you call me away, that will be the indication that my work is done in your eyes. Let your will be accomplished in us, and pour out your peace on our household.

And hear the note of miraculous victory in this prayer:

You know that all through the time of my prosperity I have been more or less consumed by a spirit of melancholy. Already you are beginning to dissipate it. I have never been happier than I am now. I have never been less sad than since you have so afflicted me!

Adolphe Monod's public ministry was over, but his new ministry was just taking shape, and God used his family to guide him into it.

The Sunday Gatherings

Once informed of the medical verdict, Adolphe's eleven siblings gathered around his sickbed. It was the first time they had all been together since the wedding of Adèle and Édouard Babut in 1822, thirty-three years earlier. Many of the siblings were living in Paris, and Billy, who had been a pastor in Rouen, was in the process of being appointed as Adolphe's suffragan pastor to take over all his duties. The 'twelve sparrows' spent the afternoons of 6 and 7 October together and celebrated the Lord's Supper. On both days, Adolphe found he was able to give a short meditation.

The success of these family services and the comments of a fellow-pastor on the value of regular communion gave rise to what came to be known as the Sunday Gatherings. Adolphe resolved to take communion each week with a small group of family and friends gathered in his bedroom. Pastors of the Reformed, Lutheran, Independent, and Wesleyan churches took turns presiding.

> *The service was celebrated in the patient's bedroom. A table placed near the bed held the bread and the cup. The officiating pastor took his place in front of the table, while Mr Monod's family with a small number of friends occupied the places around him. An effort was made to vary the group and thus to receive, in turn, all those who had asked to come. An invocation, a song, a prayer, the distribution of the elements — such was the order of service. When the Lord's Supper had been served, Mr Monod would begin to speak.*

His words were simple but eloquent. In the midst of unremitting and often excruciating pain, he spoke not about dying, and only briefly about suffering. His focus, as always, was on living wholeheartedly for Christ for whatever time remained for him or his listeners.

The services began on 14 October 1855 and continued for six long months, as the cancer slowly depleted the speaker's strength and intensified his pain. At first, not knowing how long his suffering would last, Monod chose the topics for his

Adolphe Monod on his sickbed

meditations as they came to him during the course of the week. Later, as his agony was prolonged, he began to organize the meditations into logical series. The first, *A Dying Man's Regrets*, dealt with some of the fundamentals of the Christian life: seeking God's will, prayer, studying the Bible, the use of time, and keeping our focus. The standard he set for himself and his audience was high, yet also biblical and definitely appealing. The second series, *Results*, was designed to leave a clear record of the substance of his faith on such matters as sin, the dual nature of Christ, the Scriptures, God's provision for us in Jesus Christ and through the Holy Spirit, and the Trinity.

After the first weekly service, his children decided to write down his messages. That week they combined their memories to arrive at a complete text, while on subsequent weeks, they all took notes. Adolphe was initially unaware that his words were being recorded, and he reviewed only one of the manuscripts, declaring himself to be astonished at how faithfully it captured his remarks. Each week the written text was sent to the Evangelical Church of Lyon, which Adolphe had founded.

The complete volume of twenty-five meditations was published less than a month after his death under the title, *Les Adieux d'Adolphe Monod à Ses Amis et à l'Église* (*Adolphe Monod's Farewells to his Friends and the Church*). The first printing was soon exhausted and a number of subsequent printings followed in rapid succession. Of all Monod's works, *Les Adieux* is probably the best known. It is a unique work of great depth and power, a timeless classic that has been translated many times into various languages. It has doubtless touched more lives than any of his beloved and compelling sermons. In the meditation from 13 January, he said, 'Through the suffering and afflictions he has sent me and through the hope of the eternal life that must follow them, the Lord has me exercising a different ministry. It is probably more important than the one I had proposed for myself and is, in any case, more certain because it comes to me more directly from the hand of God, who mercifully constrains me to walk in that path for his service and for his glory.' He was correct, and probably more so than he realized. *Les Adieux* was the 'enduring monument for [God's] glory' that he had wanted to leave behind.

Pastoral concerns

Between the Sunday Gatherings, there were other things to occupy Adolphe Monod. One was practical preparations for his departure. He began to set his affairs in order. He was particularly concerned for his unpublished manuscripts, leaving instructions as to how they should be handled. He also prepared to oversee the printing of one of his sermons and completed the composition of the poem or hymn entitled *Jesus Christ Rising from the Dead*, which he had begun three years earlier on one of his summer trips. He requested that Billy be appointed as his official suffragan, having previously ascertained that the small differences in their views on non-essentials of the faith would not be a problem.

All of those matters, while important, were administrative. His pastor's heart continued to beat. Each evening saw a time of family worship that began with the reciting of a hymn or Bible passage. Then Monod would give a few words and a prayer, or, if his suffering was too acute, just a prayer, often entreating the Lord for others whom he knew to be suffering. He also continued to correspond with friends, relatives, and former students, sometimes offering advice or expressing care and concern. Nine days before his death, he dictated a letter to his nephew, Henri Babut, who had fallen ill while serving as a military chaplain in Crimea. Henri had died five days before, but word had not yet reached Paris.

Another letter addressed to three dear friends is self-explanatory.

> *There are three friends whose names I like to link together for the considerable part all three played, in different times and ways, in the conversion of my soul. I want to bear witness to them of my gratitude. ... They are Louis Gaussen [his cousin in Geneva], Charles Scholl [pastor of the French church in London] and Thomas Erskine. The first worked slowly on my spirit through his gracious interactions, his preaching, his example, and his godly conversations in Satigny. The second presented the gospel to me in shorter conversations, in such a kind and*

practical, yet also wise and true way, that he won my heart. The third, uprooted my intellectual prejudices in Geneva by reconciling the gospel with sound philosophy in my mind; then in Naples he finished this work, to the extent it depends on man, by shedding light on my melancholy … through the contrast with his deep peace and tender charity. …

These three friends were not the only ones to labour for my soul. … Yet [they] were called by God to exert a combined influence on me in which they complemented one another, without knowing it. I begin by giving glory to God, and then I tell them of the love for them that fills my heart.

A single copy of this letter was circulated to the three men named, and each, in turn, wrote a touching reply. The contents of the replies were different, just as the three men and their roles in Adolphe's life were different, but each letter was filled with deep love for the invalid and for his God and with the sure expectation of a reunion in glory.

The legacy

The end of earthly life came for Adolphe Monod on Sunday 6 April 1856. All through his last illness, a group of young men, mostly medical students, had faithfully given up their own rest to spend the nights with him so that his family could sleep. The invalid was always ready to express his gratitude to them; now their care was no longer needed. The last of the Sunday Gatherings had taken place the previous week, with Adolphe giving the prayer of thanksgiving quoted at the beginning of this biography. As his strength ebbed in the ensuing days, his family wondered if they should cancel the service for 6 April, but the Lord took the ailing pastor home before the appointed hour for the gathering. Monod had often prayed that his life would not end before his ministry or his ministry before his life. God granted that request.

The funeral service was held two days later. Adolphe Monod was held in such genuine affection that more than a thousand people from all classes of society crowded into and around the funeral home in a torrential downpour and more than a hundred carriages and numerous pedestrians followed his earthly remains to the cemetery. All the pastors from both the national and independent churches were part of the procession. He shares a common grave monument with his parents, and the face that bears his name has this inscription:

ADOLPHE MONOD
PASTOR OF THE REFORMED CHURCH
BORN IN COPENHAGEN
21 JANUARY 1802
DIED IN PARIS — 6 APRIL 1856
DEATH HAS BEEN DESTROYED BY
VICTORY.
1 Cor. 15:54

After Adolphe's death, Billy continued to serve the church in Paris faithfully for eighteen years, becoming a titular pastor in 1865. Their younger brother Gustave observed, 'In my brotherly love, I liked to see in him a successor to Saint John, just as I saw in Adolphe a successor to Saint Paul.'

Tomb of Adolphe Monod and his parents

For many, Adolphe Monod seemed like a man of paradoxes. He was humble, yet bold. He started an independent church in Lyon, yet remained in the national church in Paris while others left to form a new denomination. His early preaching spoke much about sin and its penalties, while his later preaching emphasized God's love and the delight we find in following him wholeheartedly. Looking more closely, however, his life had a remarkable consistency founded on his devotion to God and his desire to see renewal brought to the Reformed Church of France. His faith was born of the

Awakening, and he consecrated his abilities to proclaiming its message — God's message — to all who would listen. In doing so, he was bold where Scripture is clear, yet humble before God and before the mysteries he has chosen not to clarify for us. He started an independent church only when fired from his previous position, and he returned to the national church when invited to do so. The emphasis of his sermons changed with the times and with his own growing maturity, but the basic message remained the same — the simple message of the gospel.

A week before his death Adolphe Monod said, 'I have a Saviour! He has freely saved me through his shed blood, and I want it to be known that I lean uniquely on that poured out blood. All my righteous acts, all my works which have been praised, all my preaching that has been appreciated and sought after — all that is in my eyes only filthy rags.'

Further reading

Adolphe Monod, *Living in the Hope of Glory* (Philipsburg NJ, P&R Publishing, 2002), Constance K. Walker, editor and translator. A new edition of Monod's *Les Adieux*, the classic collection of the short meditations he gave to family and friends during his last illness.

Adolphe Monod, *An Undivided Love: Loving and Living for Christ* (Vestavia Hills AL, Solid Ground Christian Books, 2009), Constance K. Walker, editor and translator. A collection of seven of Monod's most famous and beloved sermons. The three parts relate to finding our fulfilment in God, knowing God better, and resting happily in him and in his plan for our lives. Of the four books of Monod's sermons that I have translated, this is probably my favourite, since it speaks so directly to my heart.

Adolphe Monod, *Jesus Tempted in the Wilderness* (Vestavia Hills, AL, Solid Ground Christian Books, 2010), Constance K. Walker, editor and translator. A monograph on gaining victory over temptation. Originally given to seminary students, the three messages in this book were later adapted for the Paris pulpit but restored to their original form for publication. They unfold the nature of our battle with Satan's forces, our assurance of victory, and the weapons we use in the battle.

Adolphe Monod, *Woman: Her Mission and Her Life* (Vestavia Hills, AL, Solid Ground Christian Books, 2011), Constance K. Walker, editor and translator. This new edition of a classic work contains added material on four women from Monod's family, showing how their lives exemplify the principles set forth in the sermons.

Adolphe Monod, *Saint Paul: Changing our World for Christ* (Vestavia Hills AL, Solid Ground Christian Books, 2012). The purpose of these five discourses was to raise up a generation of young Christians who, by adopting Paul's spirit, would be effective in bringing renewal to the church and, through her, to society.

James L. Osen, *Prophet and Peacemaker: The Life of Adolphe Monod* (Lanham MD, University Press of America, 1984). A formal academic work, abounding with facts about Monod's life but lacking in understanding of his faith.

Sources

Sarah Monod, *Adolphe Monod: Souvenirs de sa Vie, Extraits de sa Correspondance* (Paris, Librairie Fischbacher, 1885). The classic work on Adolphe Monod's life. Compiled by his children, in part for the benefit of his grandchildren, it relies heavily on extracts from correspondence and diaries.
Adolphe Monod: Choix de Lettres à Sa Famille et à Ses Amis (Paris, Librairie Fischbacher, 1885). The companion volume for *Souvenirs*, containing additional correspondence both to and from Adolphe Monod.

James L. Osen, *Prophet and Peacemaker: The Life of Adolphe Monod* (Lanham MD, University Press of America, 1984). A comprehensive though fairly dry academic work. It provided many valuable references to primary sources plus details of Monod's life taken from unpublished correspondence.

Gustave Monod, *La Famille Monod: Portraits et Souvenirs* (Paris, 1890). Gustave Monod, a retired physician and younger brother of Adolphe Monod wrote this intimate account of his parents, himself, and siblings. It contains a number of priceless details, supplementing the material in *Souvenirs*, particularly with regard to Adolphe's childhood and the lives of his brothers and sisters.

Boris Decorvet and Emile G. Léonard, *Esquisse Biographique* in Adolphe Monod, *Les Adieux* (Annemasse, France, Éditions des Groupes Missionnaires, 1956). This biographical 'sketch' was my first acquaintance with the story of Adolphe Monod's life. Written on the hundredth anniversary of his death, it is a sensitive account, whose authors understood and were in harmony with Monod's faith.

Julien Monod, François Monod, and Bernard Monod, eds, *Cent Cinquante Ans Après, 1793 – 18 Janvier – 1943, Choix de Lettres et Documents* (Paris, 1943). A memorial book, written on the 150th anniversary of the wedding of Adolphe Monod's parents. It contains supplementary material and pictures relevant to the family history.

Paul Stapfer, *La Grande Prédication en France: Bossuet, Adolphe Monod* (Paris, Librairie Fischbacher, 1898). Paul Stapfer was one of Adolphe Monod's nephews, and also one of his admirers. A professor of literature in Bordeaux, he examines the sermons of Adolphe Monod and Jacques-Bénigne Bossuet, France's pre-eminent Protestant and Roman Catholic preachers, in the context of the genre of sermons. In the process, he also gives a brief account of Monod's life. Bossuet preached in the seventeenth century; Monod in the nineteenth.

Adolphe Monod, *Sermons, Deuxième Édition, Première Série* (Paris, Librairie de Charles Meyrueis, 1855). Sermons from Adolphe Monod's time as a pastor in Naples and Lyon. These sermons and those in the following three volumes were edited by Monod himself prior to publication. Each of the four volumes is around four hundred pages in length.

Adolphe Monod, *Sermons, Deuxième Édition, Deuxième Série* (Paris, Librairie de Charles Meyrueis, 1857). Sermons from Monod's time as a seminary professor in Montauban.

Adolphe Monod, *Sermons, Deuxième Édition, Troisième Série, I et II* (Paris, Librairie de Charles Meyrueis, 1859,1860). Two volumes of sermons from Monod's time as a pastor in Paris.

Adolphe Monod, *Les Adieux d'Adolphe Monod à ses Amis et à l'Église* (Paris, Librairie de Charles Meyrueis, 1856). The first edition of Adolphe Monod's death-bed meditations. These little gems, filled with life and peace and even joy, encapsulate the author's spiritual legacy.

Adolphe Monod, *Considérations sur la Nature de l'Inspiration des Apôtres* (Geneva, 1824). Adolphe Monod's seminary thesis.

Adolphe Monod, *La Destitution d'Adolphe Monod* (Paris, Librairie de Charles Meyrueis, 1864). Adolphe Monod's notes on the circumstances leading up to his dismissal from the Reformed Church of Lyon in 1832. They were published posthumously by his children.

Adolphe Monod, *Appel aux Chrétiens de France et de l'Étranger en Faveur de l'Église Évangélique de Lyon* (Paris, April 1833). A forty-page pamphlet describing the first year in the life of the Evangelical Church of Lyon and the congregation's needs for its second year of operation.

Adolphe Monod, *Explication de l'Épître aux Éphésiens* (Librairie de Charles Meyrueis, 1864). Edited notes from his teachings on Paul's Letter to the Ephesians given during the Sunday afternoon chapel services in Montauban.

Adolphe Monod, *Lucile, ou la Lecture de la Bible* (Paris, L.R. Delay, Librairie-Editeur, 1841). Monod's famous fictional work of apologetics. Its goals were to encourage everyone, but especially Roman Catholics, to read the Scriptures and to help Protestants better understand the issues involved in reaching their Catholic neighbours.

Adolphe Monod, *Pourquoi Je Demeure dans l'Église Établie* (Paris, Librairie Protestante, 1849). A public explanation of why he remained in the established, national church when his brother Frédéric and a number of other evangelicals left to form the Union of Free Evangelical Churches.

Edmond de Pressensé, *Études Contemporaines* (Paris, Librairie Sandoz et Fischbacher, 1880). The first part of this volume emphasizes the contemporary crisis in the Roman Catholic Church; the second part focuses on the Protestant church. One of the three chapters in the second part is devoted to Adolphe Monod and highlights his role in the theological renewal arising from the nineteenth-century francophone Awakening.

Marc Boegner, *Adolphe Monod, Prédicateur de l'Église Réformée* (Paris: Éditions Berger-Levrault, 1956). A talk given at the Church of the Oratoire in Paris on the one hundredth anniversary of Adolphe Monod's death.

Chants Chrétiens (Paris: J.-J. Risler, Libraire, 1834); Deuxième Édition, (1837). The first two editions of a hymnal containing Adolphe Monod's classic hymn.

Hymnes et Cantiques, song number 90, posted on http://www.cantiquest.org gives the score of the Bost melody for Monod's hymn.

J. C. Harrison, 'Reminiscences of Adolphe Monod, the Great French Preacher', *Evangelical Magazine and Missionary Chronicle*, vol. III, new series, 1861. Harrison gave his reminiscences in a series of monthly articles published in February, March, April and May. The March issue was unavailable.